THE SELF-ESTEEM
T E A C H E R

THE SELF-ESTEEM
T E A C H E R

ROBERT BROOKS, Ph.D.

Foreword by
GERARD A. POTTEBAUM
Director, Seeds of Self-Esteem Project

SEEDS OF SELF-ESTEEM
A Treehaus Production

AMERICAN GUIDANCE SERVICE
Circle Pines, Minnesota 55014-1796

© 1991 Treehaus Communications, Inc.
ISBN 0-88671-418-4
Library of Congress Catalog Card Number 91-71931

Printed and bound in the United States of America.

Book and cover design, layout and typesetting by
Treehaus Communications, Inc.
Loveland, OH 45140

AGS®
American Guidance Service
4201 Woodland Road
Circle Pines, MN 55014-1796

A   0   9   8   7   6   5   4   3   2   1

Dedication

In loving memory of my parents, Eva and David—
my first self-esteem teachers

Acknowledgments

I would like to thank many individuals whose thoughts, encouragement, and support have contributed to this book. First, to Gerard Pottebaum, president of Treehaus Communications. Jerry shares my vision of education and was instrumental in launching the *Seeds of Self-Esteem* project. His keen comments about the ideas expressed in this book were invaluable to me—in the processs of our working together, he has become a close friend. To Jane Ward, a collaborator in the *Seeds of Self-Esteem* project, my thanks for all of your input and courage throughout the project.

Next, my gratitude to colleagues and trainees at McLean Hospital. McLean Hospital provides a climate that challenges its members to develop new ideas and practices to meet the mental health needs of our society. Dr. Steven Mirin, General Director and Acting Psychiatrist-in-Chief of McLean Hospital, and Dr. Silvio Onesti, Director of the Hall-Mercer Center for Children and Adolescents of McLean Hospital, have been instrumental in promoting this climate.

Thanks also are due to two friends and colleagues, Drs. Kalman Heller and Ethan Pollak. Kal, Ethan, and I have known each other for a quarter of a century, and during that time we have shared many thoughts about children and their families—thoughts that have helped to shape my views about self-esteem.

Two individuals deserve special mention and appreciation for the role they have played in my career. Their ideas about children and education permeate this book. I first met

Dr. Sebastiano Santostefano, director of the Department of Child and Adolescent Psychology and Psychoeducation at McLean Hospital, when I began graduate school at Clark University. In the ensuing years he has served as a teacher, supervisor, and colleague who has taught me so much about understanding and communicating with children. Dr. Melvin D. Levine, Professor of Pediatrics at the University of North Carolina School of Medicine, and I began our collaboration when he was at the Children's Hospital Medical Center in Boston. Mel's visions about children and adolescents, and his wonderful respect for the unique qualities we all possess, have been a source of knowledge and inspiration for me.

To my sons, Richard and Douglas, thanks for all of the opportunities you have given me to learn about child development, education, and the vital role that self-esteem plays in each person's life. Your love, your humor, and your smiles have added so much energy to my life.

To my wife, Marilyn, my companion and friend, thank you for always being there, and for your ongoing encouragement and love.

And finally, to all of the educators I have been privileged to meet, thank you for your observations, your insights about teaching, and your dedication to your students. Your ideas about what is involved in being a self-esteem teacher may be found on each page of this book.

Robert Brooks, Ph.D.

Foreword

The Self-Esteem Teacher is the primary sourcebook in a
family of publications entitled *Seeds of Self-Esteem*. The
other components include: a four-part video series based
upon *The Self-Esteem Teacher*, featuring real school
situations to illustrate the commentary of Dr. Brooks;
twenty-seven posters that illustrate nine strategies teachers
can use to nurture self-esteem in students from
kindergarten to junior high; and *The Self-Esteem Teacher's
Journal*, a guide in which the author, Jane Ward, with
contributions from Dr. Brooks, invites teachers into teaching
experiences that liberate both teachers and students to
respect and trust those inner, unseen resources where
self-esteem takes root and flourishes from within the human
spirit.

"Listen also for what goes unsaid," a wise author once
wrote, "and you'll hear the simple truth."

Curriculum development is like that. Illusive. Often what
appears in texts is not what students learn. Some educators
call this the "hidden" curriculum—what students learn
when we're teaching them something else.

Instilling self-esteem is equally illusive. Only the theory
of self-esteem can be taught; the simple truth of self-esteem
comes from within. That is why the message Dr. Brooks
sensitively expresses in *The Self-Esteem Teacher* lies beyond
these pages.

It lies within *you*, the teacher.

The *teacher* shapes the hidden curriculum. *You* are the
unforgotten lesson students learn, the unspoken truth of all
that is said about schools and schooling.

With an ear for what goes unsaid, read between the lines of *The Self-Esteem Teacher*. You'll likely discover there, for instance, a disarming simplicity. That is not just the author's personality or professionalism coming through, as skilled as Bob Brooks is at making obvious those otherwise obtuse teacher-student interactions.

You'll find between the lines those hidden qualities—the simple, silent truth—of the self-esteem teacher. Simplicity, as I mentioned, is one. (To describe others would interfere with your own discoveries.)

Bob has often expressed delight at how teachers have found some of his simplest suggestions so effective. Simplicity is the silent partner in Bob's approach to nurturing self-esteem: to make the instilling of self-esteem *not* another addition to an overburdened curriculum but a natural part—that unspoken lesson—of everything teachers do and of everything students learn. That is the simple truth of *The Self-Esteem Teacher* and of the entire *Seeds of Self-Esteem* project.

I single out simplicity for still another reason. Simplicity frees us from pretending. It enables us to experience the wonder of ourselves and others. The joy of such freedom liberates not only students but teachers as well—from within—from that quiet center in each of us where we move in harmony with all humanity.

Gerard A. Pottebaum
Project Director

Contents

Acknowledgments iv

Foreword vi

CHAPTER 1: *Self-Esteem in the Classroom:* 1
Some Basic Questions

CHAPTER 2: *Indelible Memories of School:* 7
The Impact of Teachers on Students

CHAPTER 3: *Empathy: To See the World* 14
Through the Eyes of Another Person

CHAPTER 4: *Attribution Theory and Self-Esteem:* 27
Implications for the Classroom and School

CHAPTER 5: *Self-Esteem: Why Are We All* 33
So Different?

CHAPTER 6: *Self-Esteem Strategies:* 42
A Few Preliminary Remarks

CHAPTER 7: *To Establish an Alliance:* 47
Creating a Sense of Identity and Belonging

CHAPTER 8: *To Establish an Alliance:* 55
Understanding, Respecting, and "Joining"
the Coping Strategies of Our Students

CHAPTER 9: *To Create a "Psychological Space"*   66

CHAPTER 10: *To Offer Encouragement and*   75
    Avoid a "Praise Deficit"

CHAPTER 11: *To Develop Responsibility and*   84
    Make a Contribution

CHAPTER 12: *To Learn from Mistakes and Failure*   93

CHAPTER 13: *To Provide Choices and*   100
    Reinforce a Sense of Ownership

CHAPTER 14: *To Provide Opportunities*   107
    for Problem Solving and Decision Making

CHAPTER 15: *To Establish Self-Discipline:*   115
    The Benefits of Constructive Guidelines
    and Consequences

CHAPTER 16: *Concluding Remarks*   124

Footnotes   126

Bibliography   134

Chapter One

SELF-ESTEEM
IN THE CLASSROOM:
SOME BASIC QUESTIONS

"As a first-grade student, I had the responsibility of raising and lowering the coat closet doors because I was one of the taller boys in the class. This made me feel good because I was self-conscious about my height."

"In elementary school, I asked a question and the teacher said, 'Weren't you listening? I just answered that!' I rarely asked questions after that."

If you were asked to recall one positive and one negative experience that you had with a teacher when you were a student, what memories would be evoked? Please think about that for just a moment. I have collected hundreds of these memories from educators on a questionnaire. The responses, as illustrated by the quotes above, have been very revealing and thought-provoking. They have prompted me to ask several questions. Do teachers rely on their own vivid childhood memories of school as guideposts for planning current educational programs? Do teachers, as they interact with students, reflect upon what situations in school reinforced or lowered their self-esteem when they were youngsters? Do most educators call upon their images of childhood and adolescence in order to become what we are labeling "self-esteem teachers," taking as a high priority the fostering of a student's self-esteem?

I believe that if we use our childhood memories as important sources of information, we will find that reinforcing a student's self-esteem should be a main focus and goal in school alongside the teaching of academic and learning skills. When I have advanced this belief in my workshops, teachers have frequently posed several important questions:

• What exactly do we mean by self-esteem? What is involved in this concept?

• If we concentrate on self-esteem, is there a danger of reinforcing self-centeredness and conceit in our students?

• Is positive self-esteem associated with greater motivation and success in school?

• If we focus on reinforcing a student's self-esteem, will it take time away from teaching academic skills? Also, will we add more work to an already busy schedule?

• Even if we use strategies in the classroom to foster self-esteem, will our efforts really make a difference in the lives of our students? Don't students already have a certain self-image by the time they enter kindergarten? Do we truly have an impact, especially on those students who enter school with very low self-esteem?

My responses follow.

Self-Esteem: A Definition and a Focus

For a moment, ask yourself how you would define self-esteem. To clarify this definition, think about a couple of students whose self-esteem you would rate as high and a couple you would rate as low. What behaviors do they display that led you to judge them as you did? Were some of these behaviors more dominant than others in influencing your choices? Or, perhaps, reflect upon experiences from your own life. Select one situation in which you felt competent and proud and another time in which you did not. What was involved in each situation?

Later in this book I plan to describe a particular framework for understanding self-esteem that I have found very useful. Different researchers, educators, and mental health professionals have offered a variety of definitions of self-esteem.[1] Many of these definitions or conceptualizations overlap and focus on what individuals think and feel about themselves and about their abilities to meet certain challenges and accomplish certain tasks. Some definitions are predicated on the belief that self-esteem is the difference between our "ideal self," or how we would like to be, versus how we actually perceive ourselves. The larger the difference between our perceived self and our ideal self, the lower our self-esteem and confidence.

Yet, definitions that place too much of the spotlight on how we think and feel about ourselves can prompt some people to confuse self-esteem with self-centeredness and conceit. That is why I appreciate the more expanded definition of self-esteem offered by the California Task Force to Promote Self-Esteem and Personal and Social Responsibility in their report, *Toward a State of Esteem*. This group defined self-esteem not only in terms of "appreciating my own worth and importance," but they added "having the character to be accountable for myself and to act responsibly toward others."[2] This last part of the definition clearly embraces the view that self-esteem can never be divorced from the way we behave toward others.

Self-esteem may be seen as based upon the feelings and thoughts that individuals possess about their sense of competence and worth, about their abilities to make a difference, to meet and overcome challenges, to learn from both success and failure, and to view themselves and others with dignity and respect. Obviously, these feelings and thoughts guide our actions in different situations, and, in turn, the outcome of these actions influences our feelings and thoughts. The results can be the establishment of either damaging cycles of low self-esteem and the avoidance of challenges, or energetic cycles of high self-esteem and the confrontation of challenges.

Important questions face educators: How do we create a climate in school that helps establish positive rather than negative cycles? How do we pinpoint those areas in which each child and adolescent feels competent and then use and build upon these particular areas in school as a foundation for reinforcing self-esteem and learning? Answering these questions is a major focus of this book.

Self-Esteem: A Foundation for Motivation and Achievement

Although most of us would agree that self-esteem is a very important feature of an individual's life, educators are justified in asking whether self-esteem plays a noteworthy role in the motivation and achievement of students. Increasing evidence shows that self-esteem is significantly implicated in how motivated and successful students are in school.[3]

On the surface, there seem to be exceptions to this last statement. I am certain we all know individuals who lack confidence and yet have achieved in school. In my clinical practice, I have worked with adults whose school records were marked by success, yet they continue to harbor many doubts about their abilities. Such individuals often expend much energy to hide from others what they perceive to be their inadequacies; they experience little joy even when they succeed, always fearful that their "masquerade" of competency will abruptly be revealed.

These exceptions notwithstanding, in most instances the greater a student's self-esteem and confidence, the greater the probability that the student possesses a high level of motivation to persevere and succeed. Very importantly, when a student succeeds, the student experiences a sense of genuine accomplishment and satisfaction rather than continued self-doubt and anxiety about being able to achieve in the future. Such a student is willing to take risks and learn from, rather than feel defeated by, failure. I believe that recognition of this link between self-esteem and success in school has contributed to the expanding interest in strategies for reinforcing self-esteem in the classroom.

Fostering Self-Esteem in the Classroom:
Adding Another Curriculum?

I have provided workshops for thousands of teachers, and I am well aware of their many responsibilities and their busy—sometimes overwhelming—schedules. For example, with the increased number of children from single-parent homes or homes in which both parents work full-time, teachers have told me that in addition to their other duties, they feel they are being asked to assume the role of a surrogate parent. Also, in order to develop good relationships with parents, they must accommodate parents' hectic schedules, often at the expense of spending time with their own families.

Teachers question if the use of strategies to promote student self-esteem will take valuable time away from teaching academic tasks, if it will require the learning and implementing of an entirely new curriculum, or if it will add time to an already overbooked schedule. I recognize that there is a limit to what anyone can accomplish in the classroom. Certainly, it is not my intention to advocate the introduction of additional educational material and strategies that, although valuable, will represent the "straw that broke the camel's back."

It is true that some time will be necessary to learn the principles and strategies discussed in this book. However, once this initial learning takes place, the use of strategies to foster self-esteem in the classroom does not need to take time away from academic tasks nor need it add time to a teacher's schedule. Rather, the goal is for self-esteem strategies to become blended with the teaching of academic skills, so that a classroom atmosphere is developed that makes teaching and learning more exciting and satisfying for both educators and students. Such excitement can lessen the stresses and burdens that many teachers experience and contribute to the "classroom magic" discussed by

Louise DeFelice in the following passage:

> Perhaps one of the reasons that we don't get around to
> covering the topic of classroom magic is because it's not a
> measurable phenomenon. It's elusive and mercurial,
> something felt rather than seen. However, we have all
> experienced magic in the form of a palpable sense of vitality
> that seems to energize everything and everyone in the
> classroom. Sometimes it's a bubbling, exuberant kind of
> energy. Other times it's a powerful, quiet kind of energy.
> Either kind transforms lessons into learning and creates the
> charged atmosphere in which we also become transformed.
> Our perceptions shift, and we comprehend significant things
> about the world outside us and the world inside us.[4]

If we accept the beliefs that positive self-esteem is
associated with success in school and that teachers have
effective strategies available to reinforce the self-esteem of
students, we now turn to the fifth question posed earlier,
namely, even when using these strategies, do teachers truly
have a long-lasting impact on the lives of their students,
including those who enter school with a very poor
self-image? The answer to this question touches on the very
heart of this book.

Chapter Two

INDELIBLE MEMORIES OF SCHOOL: THE IMPACT OF TEACHERS ON STUDENTS

"In the first grade, I was a helper in assisting another student to learn to read. I have never forgotten this."

"I especially remember my third-grade teacher. She realized I was shy but capable. She let me help other students with their reading. I felt great. She gave me many responsible classroom jobs—organizing cupboards, etc. From grade three, I wanted to be an elementary teacher— and I am. This third-grade teacher was good to everyone."

It is meaningless to discuss strategies for fostering the self-esteem of students unless teachers believe that what they do in the classroom makes a difference in the lives of those they are teaching. When we consider the question of the impact that teachers have, we are also addressing the issue of the self-esteem of teachers. When people believe that what they are doing is of little consequence, their self-esteem in that situation will not be reinforced; their motivation and energy will be minimal, and they cannot help but convey this to others. When those others are students, what will result is a learning environment devoid of excitement and purpose and filled with boredom and perhaps anger. Thus, reinforcing students' self-esteem can never truly be separated from teachers' self-esteem.

Back to the question: Do you believe you can have a long-lasting impact on your students? Five, ten, twenty years from now, will your students remember you or experiences from your class? And, if so, what do you hope they remember? These kinds of questions prompted me to develop the anonymous questionnaire I referred to in the previous chapter. On this one-page questionnaire, I asked educators to respond to the four questions listed below. As you read each question, ask yourself how you would respond.

1. Please describe briefly one experience that you had with an educator when you were a student that reinforced your self-esteem. What grade were you in at the time?

2. Please describe briefly one experience that you had with an educator when you were a student that lessened your self-esteem. What grade were you in at the time?

3. Please list a couple of things that enhance your effectiveness and self-esteem as an educator.

4. Please list a couple of things that lessen your effectiveness and self-esteem as an educator.

At this point, I want to concentrate on teachers' responses to the first two questions. Perhaps as important as what they wrote on the questionnaire were the emotions that were triggered as they recalled past school experiences. In my workshops, I have been impressed by the number of teachers who want to talk about their past experiences and who have shared with me how recent the memories seem, even though for some these memories are more than fifty years old. The memories live on, continuing to play a role in our lives even if we are not certain what their influence is—they are indeed indelible memories, indicative of the lifelong influence that a teacher can have.

I was curious what images from the past my questionnaire would elicit. My curiosity was not simply academic, for I felt that if we discovered certain themes emerging from these vivid memories, these same themes might be equally relevant for students in today's world. Might not our memories guide us in providing experiences that could someday become the indelible positive memories of our current students? And might they not also guide us to avoid situations that could become negative memories?

At the beginning of the first two chapters I offered several examples of these memories. I believe some additional teacher responses would be useful. As you read these, ask yourself: Why would one of my colleagues in the teaching profession select *this* memory from all of the other possible memories? What makes this memory so powerful? What can I learn from it in terms of my own teaching style?

The Indelible Memories of Educators: The Positive Side

What follows is a representative sample of positive memories:

"I remember an exceptional American history teacher in high school during my junior year. I was impressed with his love of the subject and his teaching talent. He went out of his way throughout the year to encourage me to speak up in class. He sensed that I was shy, so, in measured steps and with great skill, he asked more and more of me in terms of participating and projecting in discussions. He believed in me and gently pushed me to face what I found hardest to do—speak in the public arena. I will never forget him."

"In the third grade, I was chosen to help get the milk and straws. In the fifth grade, I was given a major part in a school show."

"My sixth-grade teacher chose me to collect banking money from class members, keep records, and take the money to the bank. It made me feel competent and responsible."

"My seventh-grade math teacher asked me to thoroughly explain a homework assignment on the board."

"My fifth-grade teacher pulled me aside and asked if I would prepare a presentation for the class."

"In eleventh grade I was struggling with composition. A new English teacher took the time to point out that there were some good things in my writing. It motivated me to work harder on my themes, and before the year was out I had received my first 'A minus' on a composition. I still have that composition."

"In the fourth grade, my teacher let me run the film projector (thread, rewind, etc.). I was otherwise very rambunctious during films."

"I had a teacher in junior high who knew that I was particularly shy. She would never challenge me and ask me to answer publicly, but instead took me aside and said, 'I can tell by your knowing glance and your facial expressions that you are participating silently and that you know the answers.' "

"In the fourth grade, I was asked to paint a mural along with three other students to be a permanent part of the school. It was wonderfully positive! Later, as an eighth-grade teacher, I had a class paint a mural on a 1783 colonial farm in Connecticut."

"In the sixth grade, the children in my class and my teacher didn't believe I could read as well or as quickly as I did. When testing proved me right, the teacher apologized in front of the class."

"I had an eighth-grade teacher who gave me the responsibility for creating the decorations/backdrops for the school programs (Christmas and spring). It was a massive undertaking. She greatly encouraged my artistic interests and talents."

The Indelible Memories of Educators: The Negative Side

Now let's examine some of the negative experiences. Again, as you read these, think about the following questions: Why were these memories selected? What are these teachers communicating? What relevance do their memories contain for me as I relate with my own students?

"It was grade eleven. Math was hard for me. I don't remember this lady's name, but she had a way of making me feel like a second-class citizen because I didn't understand things the first time. I think it wasn't specific words, but the subtle things in her tone of voice and body language that indicated how frustrated she was with my slowness."

"My third-grade teacher threw chalk at people and issued demerits for 'bad behavior.' She also gave me a 'U' (Unsatisfactory) in Posture when I had a leg cast up to my thigh."

"A teacher sneered at me."

"I was told by a grade-school teacher that my answer was stupid."

"My algebra teacher accused me of asking questions to disrupt the class, when in truth I was seeking understanding."

"In fourth grade, I had a dreadful experience. I had written a poem at home and presented it to my teacher. She put me in a room by myself and said, 'Now write one in school.' Feeling very uninspired, I did not write a poem and her reaction was, 'Well, I can see you probably did not write the first one on your own.' "

"In the sixth grade, my teacher informed me that because I was in the gifted program I would not be allowed to make any spelling mistakes. In the third grade, I held my pencil incorrectly. As I was writing, my teacher pushed my pencil the proper way and made a mess of my paper."

"My sophomore English teacher belittled all of us at one time or another. He was angry, sarcastic, bitter, and we were terrified in that classroom. I heard that he left teaching a few years later—thank God!"

"In kindergarten, on the third day of school, I was sent to the principal's office for yawning. It was a loud one, but I was only five. As we walked to the office, my teacher said, 'You'll stay here until you can control yourself. A five-year-old should know better.' "

"In the tenth grade, my geometry teacher asked if I was dumb because I didn't understand some point he was making."

The Teacher as a "Charismatic Adult"

In the process of collecting all of these memories of school, I became even more convinced that teachers have a significant impact on their students, an impact that is not transitory but will long be remembered. This conviction is shared by others. For instance, in an article titled, "Teachers Have Enormous Power in Affecting a Child's Self-Esteem," psychologist Julius Segal examines what factors help children who have grown up in homes with abuse, neglect, and chaos to overcome these conditions and develop a healthy self-image and a trust in others. Segal writes:

> From studies conducted around the world, researchers have distilled a number of factors that enable such children of misfortune to beat the heavy odds against them. One factor turns out to be the presence in their lives of a charismatic adult—a person with whom they identify and from whom they gather strength. And in a surprising number of cases, that person turns out to be a teacher.[1]

Segal also emphasizes that the teacher's "magic works in less extreme cases as well."[2] His writings are supported by psychologist Emmy Werner's thirty-five-year longitudinal study of individuals growing up on a rural island in Hawaii. Werner as well as others have used the label *resilient* to describe high-risk children who are successful as adults. In her research, Werner found that the influence of at least one adult played a significant role in helping children to be resilient.[3]

A Massachusetts Department of Education report about at-risk students supports the significant role an educator can play:

> Possibly the most critical element to success within school is a student developing a close and nurturing relationship with at least one caring adult. Students need to feel that there is someone within school whom they know, to whom they can turn, and who will act as an advocate for them.[4]

I believe that every educator is capable of becoming a self-esteem teacher, a "charismatic adult" who truly infuses students with a feeling of excitement and self-worth, who helps them see more clearly the positive in themselves and in others. And yet, so many teachers still question the impact they can have; perhaps they are so drained by the daily hassles they face in school that they lose sight of how influential they can be. As Tracy Kidder eloquently observes in his book *Among Schoolchildren*:

> Teachers usually have no way of knowing that they have made a difference in a child's life, even when they have made a dramatic one. But for children who are used to thinking of themselves as stupid or not worth talking to or deserving rape and beatings, a good teacher can provide an astonishing revelation. A good teacher can give a child at least a chance to feel, "*She* thinks I'm worth something. Maybe I am." Good teachers put snags in the river of children passing by, and over the years, they redirect hundreds of lives. Many people find it easy to imagine unseen webs of malevolent conspiracy in the world, and they are not always wrong. But there is also an innocence that conspires to hold humanity together, and it is made up of people who can never fully know the good that they have done.[5]

In accepting the belief that educators can influence and redirect lives, we must continue to ask, "What are the roads we can take with our students, and what is our final destination?" When the journey is over, what indelible memories do we hope have been stored by our students to serve as road maps for their future journeys?

I want to turn next to the journeys I embarked upon that led me to believe that the concept of self-esteem should be dominantly displayed on all of these road maps, providing us with direction and purpose.

Chapter Three

EMPATHY: TO SEE THE WORLD THROUGH THE EYES OF ANOTHER PERSON

"In kindergarten, I was so afraid of leaving my mom. I was terrified being at school. I can remember how gentle the teacher was, allowing me to feel, letting me join at my own pace. After that year, I always wanted to become a teacher of young children. I now teach second grade."

"A teacher gave me a book in the third grade with an inscription in it, 'To a little girl who loves to read.'"

I have been asked on several occasions when it was that I first became interested in the concept of self-esteem, what it was that prompted my interest, and whether this concept has always guided my work. The answers to these questions are rooted in my early experiences as a psychologist and as a parent. I want to share some of these experiences since they serve to illustrate several central thoughts about self-esteem.

The Experiences of a Young Psychologist and Parent

Not surprisingly, when I first began graduate school, there were few, if any, principles that directed my clinical interventions. As much as I wanted to be a therapist, I found the initial experience disconcerting. I still remember that after a few weeks of seeing patients—some children, some adults—I said to myself, "Bob, if you're really honest, you have to admit you don't know what you're doing as a therapist! What are you trying to accomplish? What impact do you want to have? What are your goals?" I had no adequate answers.

I was so nervous in those beginning days that I used to say a prayer before every session. When you hear this prayer you'll be thankful you weren't one of my first patients. I used to pray that the patient not say anything important to me. (I wasn't even certain what was important.) What a prayer for a psychologist to utter! But if one doesn't know what one's own goals and objectives are, if one doesn't know what one wants to accomplish, then how can one respond intelligently and helpfully when a patient says something that sounds important? When I have informed teachers of my early anxieties, many recall their own initial doubts about their professional competence.

I struggled—I use "struggle" in the most positive sense of the word—to make sense of what I was doing as a clinician. This struggle as a beginning psychologist was soon intensified by the challenges and questions I faced as a new parent. I especially recall an experience I had when my older son, Richard, was a newborn, an experience that heightened my motivation to articulate the important ingredients involved in raising and educating children. It was truly a very powerful moment in my life.

I remember holding Richard, who is now twenty-three, when he was five days old. As I looked at him, I was flooded with the multitude of feelings that most new parents experience when they hold their newborn: joy, satisfaction, anxiety. I said to myself almost with disbelief, "This is really my child!" Suddenly, thoughts of my own infancy emerged as I imagined myself in the arms of my mother and father, wondering what their feelings were when they held me when I was five days old. Were their feelings similar to what I was experiencing with Richard?

As I continued to gaze at Richard, I thought about how over the years I had been involved with my parents in countless interactions that were very influential in determining the kind of person I had become. As a consequence of these interactions, I formed some vivid images of my parents—almost all of which were very positive. I wondered what interactions lay ahead for Richard and me. As Richard grew older, how would he respond to the kinds of questions I posed for my child and adolescent patients, questions such as: "Tell me about your father. What kind of person is he? What is one of the happiest memories you have of you and your father together? What is an unhappy memory? How does your father show you love? What makes your father proud of you? What angers your father about you? If you could change one thing about your father what would it be?" (The same kinds of questions would be just as relevant in obtaining children's perceptions of their mother and other important adults in their lives.)

Thus, just as I was engaged in the struggle to articulate what impact I would like to have on my patients, I was also prompted to reflect upon what impact I hoped to have on my son. What did I think was important in raising a child? How did I hope he would perceive me?

Empathy: The Road to Understanding

My search for answers as a psychologist and parent led me to discover the central role that self-esteem plays in each person's life. I realized that if I were to define the factors that are significant in raising and educating children, I had to become increasingly empathic and see the world more clearly through the eyes of these children. Most of us would agree, however, that while empathy is an invaluable skill when relating to others, it is often difficult to achieve. For instance, at some point in my initial meeting with parents who have come to see me because of concerns they have about one of their children, I pose several questions that directly assess empathy. Many parents have told me that these were some of the most difficult questions I raised and

yet, some of the most important since they provoked much
thought. I ask, "Describe a typical day in your child's life, but
through your child's eyes. For example, how does your child
feel when he (she) first gets up in the morning, sees you,
goes to school? How does your child feel about herself
(himself), about her (his) abilities to succeed? How does your
child experience being taught, encouraged, disciplined?"

It is not unusual for parents to tell me that they hadn't
really thought about how their child perceived things. When
they do attempt to answer my questions, their first response
often reflects the way in which they view their child rather
than how their child might see the world. As I challenge
parents to struggle with the task of entering the world of
their children, I also attempt to extend an empathic
understanding to them, to place myself inside their shoes, to
understand how they experience themselves, their children,
and their role as parents.

Encouraged by the motivation with which parents
reacted to and reflected upon my questions, I began to pose
similar kinds of questions to educators. When I visited a
school to consult with teachers involved with one of my
patients, I frequently asked how they thought my patient
felt coming into the school building each morning, being in
their class, being taught, being praised, being corrected.
Interestingly, the initial response of many teachers was
similar to that of parents—namely, that they had not really
thought about how their students perceived school or them.
My questions were not intended to turn teachers and parents
into "pseudoshrinks," poised to look for the hidden and
symbolic meanings in every behavior and communication;
rather, my goal was to heighten awareness of the inner world
of the children and adolescents with whom we interact, to
become tuned in to the feelings and thoughts that influence
their perception of themselves and others. The more we
could understand the perceptions of our children, the
greater our capacity to enhance their development.

Let me illustrate: I attended a school conference in which
teachers voiced frustration about a teenage girl who

sabotaged their best efforts to help even when she had
initially agreed to the recommended intervention. Their
annoyance and anger were understandable, but
unfortunately these feelings were interfering with
successfully planning and implementing other possible
strategies. The tenor of the meeting changed noticeably
when I asked them how they thought this student felt every
morning as she entered the school building. One of her
teachers said that he had not previously thought about that
question, but one word came to mind: "defeated." A
colleague agreed and said, "How do we help her to feel less
defeated?" A productive, problem-solving dialogue ensued
that eclipsed the frustration and anger that had existed only
moments before. The teachers had assumed a more
empathic posture.

Descriptions of Our Teachers and Ourselves

I would like to describe a brief workshop exercise. As I do,
reflect upon how you would respond. I ask those in
attendance to think about one teacher whom they really
liked when they were students. I then ask the audience to
describe that teacher. The words are very positive: "caring,"
"was interested in us," "demanding and supportive,"
"humorous," "was excited about what she taught," "made
learning fun."

Next, I ask the audience if they ever remember being
overjoyed when they were students upon learning that one of
their teachers was out sick. The question prompts laughter
but also some strong negative feelings when I request that
they describe the teacher in question. "Intimidating,"
"demeaning," "boring," "dull," "belittling," "never took
time to learn our names" are a few examples of the
descriptions I have heard.

Having called forth memories of a liked and disliked
teacher, I next say, "Imagine for a moment that I ask all of
you to leave and I call in the students you teach. I then
request your students to use one or more words to describe
you. What words would you hope they use? What words

do you think they would use? What images do you think are important to project as a teacher? If we could see the world through your students' eyes, what images would be cast?"

Portraits and Stories: Guides to Our Inner World

In my quest to be more empathic, I posed the same questions for myself that I did for parents and teachers. Whether I was doing individual or family therapy, consulting with a teacher, offering a workshop, or talking with my children, I attempted to understand how the people with whom I was interacting perceived me and what issues emerged as most important for them.

In my clinical work as I undertook evaluations of children and adolescents, I used psychological testing to help me paint a portrait of each patient, a portrait revealing features of their inner world and their perception of themselves and others.[1] I did the same when I asked students to complete brief questionnaires prior to my talking with their class. In therapy, I invited patients to write and tell stories as another vehicle through which to gain information about their world.[2]

We all have stories to tell about our lives. As I listened and watched, as I examined the different ways in which people expressed their stories through words and actions, I came to believe very strongly that a basic feature in every individual's life centered on self-esteem. The renowned psychologist Robert White advanced this view when he wrote that within every individual from birth is a drive to be effective and competent, to master one's environment.[3] Other individuals and groups have also highlighted the significant impact of self-esteem on our lives: Richard Bednar, M. Gawain Wells, and Scott Peterson in their approach to therapy; Jeanne Gibbs in the development of the Tribes program that focuses on the formation of student groups for cooperative learning; and the California Task Force to Promote Self-Esteem and Personal and Social Responsibility.[4]

The importance of self-esteem is readily captured in the following examples from my clinical practice.

Wendy, a seven-year-old second grader with attentional problems, was referred by her parents because they and Wendy's teachers were concerned about her seeming underachievement. (She tested in the superior range on the *Wechsler Intelligence Scale for Children—Revised.*[5]) They also were worried about her inattentiveness and daydreaming and poor reading skills. During my evaluation, Wendy told me that she had difficulty paying attention and reading, adding, "I get sweaty and my head buzzes when I try too long."

I used a therapeutic storytelling technique that I developed called "Creative Characters"[6] with Wendy. Since she had told me that she thought she was one of the only children in her school who had trouble paying attention, I engaged her in writing a story about her experience that I could read to children, parents, and teachers to help them understand the problem more clearly.

Wendy decided to have as the main character a dog named "Hyper" who had difficulty concentrating and learning—an obvious representation of herself. The central position of self-esteem in Wendy's life was reflected in the second paragraph of her story, a paragraph with far-reaching implications. Wendy wrote:

> Hyper told herself that she would get over this problem someday, but she wondered if she really would. She was worried that when she grew up and her own puppies asked her something, she would not know the answer and they would wonder why their mother was not very smart. Thinking about this made Hyper feel upset.

Wendy was not only portraying a picture of low self-esteem but also the fear that the situation would never improve—that she was forever destined to be "not very smart." What a powerfully upsetting image for such a young child.

A second example concerns Steven, a boy who was referred to me when he was entering high school. I have elected to discuss Steven in part because of the images of a teacher he shared with me in words and drawings. Steven presented a complicated picture of a teenager with learning disabilities who suffered bouts of depression and a lack of energy that had both physical and emotional components. At times, it was difficult for him to get to school, and when he did, he was often late. From the moment I met Steven, I was impressed by his capacity to reflect upon and make sense of his problems. I found him to be a very articulate and likable teenager.

In an attempt to gain some understanding of his problems, Steven began to write his autobiography, especially focusing on memories of teachers and school. His words revealed questions about his own self-worth. Intense feelings about a fourth-grade teacher also appeared, a teacher who apparently told Steven on many occasions that he was lazy and unmotivated. Steven felt that this teacher interpreted his slowness in learning and the questions he asked in class as a sign that he was not really interested in succeeding.

When children are told by significant adults that they are lazy and unmotivated, they typically begin to believe these judgments. The impact on their self-esteem can be devastating as is vividly captured in the following passage from Steven's autobiography, a recollection from his fourth-grade year:

> I flunked my spelling test again, and what's even worse is that this time I thought I could pass it. Instead I got nine wrong. It was probably my fault too. Maybe I didn't study hard enough because last night their were a lot of things to do. My teacher was right, I am lazy, I have no excuse. . . . Just thinking about having to spell words like congrachulashions and buteaful makes me panic.

This so-called lazy and unmotivated boy, even with the burden of his learning disabilities, possessed a wonderful style of expressing his feelings and thoughts through drawings and words. He was an impressive artist as evidenced by an award one of his paintings won in an art

contest when he was in high school—a painting that was so
good that it was displayed in an art gallery in New York City.
Given his artistic skills, he drew the three pictures depicted
in Figures 1, 2, and 3. The first drawing represents how
Steven thought his teacher saw him every day in the fourth
grade, namely, "sick in the brain." The second and third
drawings depict Steven's view of his teacher. When Steven
showed me these drawings, he guessed that his teacher
never realized how he came across to Steven or the impact
he had on Steven's self-esteem. His drawings are a testimony
to the importance of being empathic, of seeing the world
through the eyes of our students.

Figure 1

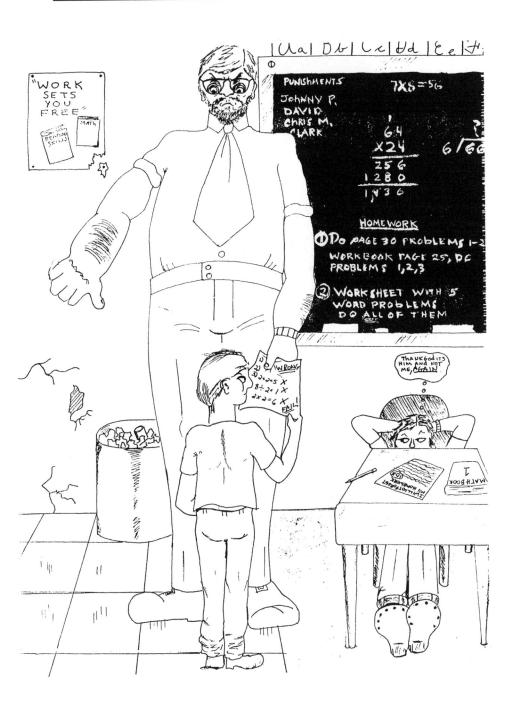

Figure 2

Figure 3

In his autobiography, Steven wrote a letter to his
fourth-grade teacher. It was never sent but captures his
experience in that class. A section of this letter is printed
below. Steven's sarcasm represents his anger and his
continuing struggles to extricate himself from the view that
he is lazy:

> I know that I myself was a pain at times, always flunking
> spelling tests and never understanding my math lessons. I just
> was irresponsible, I guess, and I didn't work hard enough. I
> should have studied for two hours instead of one and you of
> course had a perfect right to be angry and tell me I was lazy
> under those circumstances.
>
> One thing I remember vividly about your class was how
> dedicated you were to each student. You were, even to me.
> Remember how you used to yell at me to make me understand
> my math facts? I realize your motives behind that now that I
> am older. You simply were pushing to make me work harder
> and harder since I often sat through math class just staring at
> the paper. A lazy thing to do, but I didn't understand what
> went on in class. When I asked for help you had a perfect right
> to be annoyed for I should've been listening more carefully in
> the first place.

Some might argue that the stories of Wendy and Steven
and my other patients are not representative of the issues
most of us face since they were created by individuals who
are in therapy. However, while self-esteem problems may be
more pronounced in a clinical population, my experience has
been that every person struggles to a greater or lesser extent
with issues that fall under the umbrella of self-esteem. Such
everyday occurrences as adults who will not accept an
invitation to speak in public for fear of embarrassing
themselves, children who will not raise their hands to answer
a question in class for fear of making a mistake, adults and
children who exaggerate their accomplishments, or blame
others for their failures—all represent self-esteem struggles.

My growing recognition of the pervasive influence of
self-esteem led to another challenge. It was not enough to
simply advocate in a general way that self-esteem be

reinforced. Instead, I wondered if a framework existed for investigating self-esteem that could be translated into specific strategies for enhancing self-esteem at school, at home, or in therapy. I eventually found such a framework, which has proved particularly useful in guiding my interventions, including those that take place in the classroom. In the next chapter, I discuss this framework and its far-reaching implications for educators.

Chapter Four

ATTRIBUTION THEORY AND SELF-ESTEEM: IMPLICATIONS FOR THE CLASSROOM AND SCHOOL

"When doing math on the board, I made an error. The student next to me told me to copy hers. When I refused and preferred to stay with my solution, my teacher praised me because I had the 'courage of my convictions.' "

Think about two experiences that you have had, one that resulted in success, the other in failure. What factors do you believe contributed to the two outcomes? From the time we are very young children, we will encounter numerous tasks and situations that result in either success or failure. Often without realizing it, we provide reasons to ourselves to explain why we succeeded or failed. Researchers have found that these reasons vary from person to person and are strongly linked to an individual's self-esteem.

"Attribution theory," initially proposed by Bernard Weiner and applied by many clinicians and researchers in their work,[1] examines the significant differences among us in terms of the factors to which we attribute our accomplishments and our mistakes. I believe that this theory has much to offer educators, especially because it can be translated into concrete strategies for fostering self-esteem in the school.

The Successes in Our Lives

If we first look at successful experiences, the research related to attribution theory has found that, in general, children who possess high self-esteem believe that, in great part, their own efforts and ability determine their success. Children with high self-esteem mastering a two-wheel bicycle, or obtaining a high score on an exam, or getting a base hit in a Little League game, or getting along with other children, or performing impressively in a musical recital, may certainly give credit to the adults who taught and assisted them, but they will also believe that they are influential architects in determining what transpires in their lives. They take realistic credit for that which they have accomplished.

The picture is strikingly different for children and adolescents with low self-esteem. These youngsters often attribute success to luck or chance—to factors outside their control—thereby lessening their confidence that they will be capable of succeeding in the future. For example, many students with learning difficulties all too often dismiss a good test grade with such comments as, "The teacher made the test easy" or "I was lucky." Conspicuously absent is the belief that they contributed in some fashion to the success.

If students in your classroom believe that achievement is based on luck or good fortune, their motivation and self-direction will be tenuous at best. Believing that they have little, if any, control over their ability to learn, they will not invest themselves in learning tasks. These students frequently lack a sense of ownership or responsibility for that which occurs in their classrooms or their school, feeling that education is being imposed upon them. "I don't like school, but I have to go. I can't wait for the weekend so I don't have to go to school." " School is a pain." These statements reflect the minimal investment and lack of belonging that many students, especially those with poor self-esteem, have in school.

These students, burdened by low self-esteem and psychologically estranged from school, present a major challenge for educators. We must ask ourselves how we can create an environment in school that will maximize the probability that children and adolescents will not only succeed, but will also believe that their success is based on their own resources and effort. Stated somewhat differently, how do we help students feel an increasing sense of ownership and responsibility for their own education? As will become apparent later in this book, teachers can use a number of strategies from the very beginning of the school year to reinforce these feelings of student ownership and responsibility.

The Mistakes and Failures in Our Lives

Now let's turn to what attribution theory has to say about mistakes and failures. In my practice, one of the ways I assess children's self-esteem is by asking their parents and teachers how these children respond to being unsuccessful. Let's look at the following two examples: Two children in the same fourth-grade class have just failed a spelling test. Walking out of the class, one child says, "I better study more next time, maybe go for extra help. I can do better than this." The second child says, "The teacher stinks—he never told us that these words would be on the test. He should be fired!" Now let's transport ourselves to the baseball field where two ten-year-olds on the same Little League team have just struck out each time at bat. At the end of the game, one child approaches the coach and says, "Can you see what I'm doing wrong? I keep missing the ball." The other angrily throws down the bat and shouts that the umpire is blind.

The first child in each of these examples, the one who is willing to expend additional energy to study or ask the teacher or coach for assistance, entertains the belief that mistakes are experiences to learn from rather than feel defeated by. Children such as these typically have high self-esteem and attribute a lack of success—especially if the task is realistically achievable—to factors they can change, such as applying more effort or using more effective strategies or techniques.

The second child in each example typifies the kind of child who greatly frustrates parents, teachers, and psychologists as they attempt to help. This child blames someone or something for failure, believing that one does not learn from mistakes, but rather that each mistake is another rock being placed around the neck, weighing the child down more and more. Such children and adolescents perceive mistakes as resulting from conditions that cannot be easily modified, such as lack of ability or low intelligence. Feeling hopeless and wishing to avoid further perceived humiliation, they are apt to give up, offer excuses, blame others, or resort to other ineffective ways of coping, such as assuming the role of the class clown or class bully. As these students become older, our attempts to reach them are often met with angry retorts: "Leave me alone!" "I don't care!" "It's my life, I'll do what I want with it!" These children care much more than we realize, but with the feeling that they cannot improve, they wonder why they should even try.

No child is totally immune to the fears associated with making mistakes and failing, although children with low self-esteem are especially vulnerable. I believe that these fears play a role in every classroom unless they are confronted directly. Just as I raised the question of how we can help students assume an increasing sense of ownership and responsibility for their own education, I wish to raise another important question: How do we create a climate in school that reinforces in students the belief that mistakes are experiences to learn from, that mistakes are not only to be *accepted*, but also *expected*? We need to communicate to children and adolescents that they should not feel defeated by mistakes, that mistakes can serve as the basis for learning and growth. Later we will examine strategies for reinforcing this message.

The Search for Islands of Competence

I am certain we can all think of children and adolescents who are much more self-assured playing basketball or baseball than they are taking a math exam or talking with their peers, and of other youngsters who are comfortable in the classroom but very self-conscious playing a sport. As I attempt to develop interventions that will foster a sense of student ownership and assist students to handle mistakes more constructively, I use a metaphor or image that serves as a powerful source of energy and guidance for me. The metaphor is based on the recognition that an individual's self-esteem may vary from one situation to the next and that all of us feel more confident engaged in some activities than others.

If children or adolescents experience low self-esteem in many situations, especially those that they judge to be important in the eyes of significant others, their overall sense of competence will be very low. The metaphor I use to capture this feeling of inadequacy involves an image in which I see many, if not all, of my patients swimming or drowning in an ocean of self-perceived inadequacy—they have communicated to me that they believe they cannot succeed. To counteract this image of drowning, I contend that every person in this world possesses at least one small "island of competence," one area that is or has the potential to be a source of pride and achievement.

This metaphor is not intended to be merely a fanciful image, but rather a symbol of respect and hope, a reminder that all children and adolescents have areas of strength. Those who are teaching and raising children have the responsibility to find and build upon these islands of competence so that they will soon become more prominent than the ocean of self-doubt.

In the school environment, I believe it is imperative for us to find ways of displaying a student's islands of competence. If students experience school as a place where their strengths rather than their deficits are spotlighted, they are likely to be more motivated to learn and achieve. While all students deserve to have their islands of competence displayed and built upon, there is a more urgent need to do so for those students who lack confidence in their ability to learn. If we can find and reinforce the areas of strength these students possess, my experience has been that we can open the way for a "ripple effect," where students may be more willing to venture forth and confront tasks that have been problematic for them.

When we examine specific strategies for fostering self-esteem in schools and classrooms, it will become evident that islands of competence are varied and can be reinforced in many different ways. How successfully these islands are cultivated will depend upon the creativity, caring, and sensitivity of teachers. The self-esteem teacher recognizes that locating and cultivating even one island of competence can serve as the catalyst for the development of others. The discovery of each new island provides further encouragement for students to take risks and to search for islands not yet uncovered. As they venture into uncharted waters, they do so with heightened responsibility for their own actions and with a willingness to face increasingly demanding challenges, challenges from which they formerly fled. They are better equipped to face hardships and setbacks because of what they have taken from their self-esteem teachers. Learning truly becomes an exciting process, and the excitement is shared equally between student and teacher.

Chapter Five

SELF-ESTEEM: WHY ARE WE ALL SO DIFFERENT?

"A fifth-grade teacher noticed I was good in art. She taught me to paint with oils. I have always appreciated that she noticed me. I'm now an artist as well as a teacher. My mom noticed too, but to have a teacher notice was quite an honor to me."

"In sixth grade, I had trouble understanding science terms worded other than as glossary meanings. A teacher told me I could still know the answers if explained to me the way I understood them. She took the time to give me an oral science test. It boosted my confidence, and I was able to do written tests from thereafter."

I am often asked why some children develop a positive self-image while others are burdened by self-doubt and a lack of confidence. The answer is far from simple.[1] Certainly, the experiences we encounter as children—how others respond to and treat us—play a crucial role in the formation of our self-esteem, but other factors operate as well. For example, I was not surprised to find that the self-esteem of my patients who were physically and emotionally abused as children bore the deep scars of this abuse. But what of the children and adolescents who have grown up in relatively loving and

caring homes—why is it that some of them lack
self-assurance? Or what of the children who have
experienced various hardships and yet somehow have
developed a self-image permeated with feelings of confidence
and hope?

How we become who we are is indeed a very complex
picture, involving the interaction of our inborn temperament
and biological makeup with the environmental forces we
encounter as we develop. Gaining greater awareness of the
variables that shape our personalities will help us become
more realistic in recognizing the influence we can have in
fostering the self-esteem of students. Let us look first at one
of the factors that contribute to the formation of
self-esteem—inborn temperament and biological makeup.

Differences From Birth

With some embarrassment, I must confess that when I
first began my training as a psychologist I assumed that all
children were exactly the same at birth. Thus, when parents
came to see me about problems their child was experiencing,
I thought that they must have "caused" these problems, that
they were to blame—why else would their child be
encountering difficulties? How simplistic a thought! After my
oldest child, Richard, was born I said, "There's more to
parenting than meets the eye." When Douglas was born I
said, "Children are really different from birth!"

The work of two psychiatrists, Stella Chess and
Alexander Thomas, has contributed greatly to our knowledge
of child development. They found that even at birth the
temperaments of infants differ noticeably as reflected in the
ways in which they respond to their environment. For
example, some infants are more active, others less active,
some seem to have a happy mood while others appear more
negative, some are hypersensitive to touch or sound while
others are not, and some quickly develop regular eating and
sleeping schedules while others never do.

Given variations in the temperamental patterns of
children they studied, Chess and Thomas provided labels for

three kinds of children: the easy child, the slow-to-warm-up child, and the difficult child.[2] They note that these are not precise labels since not all children fit into any of these three groups, while other youngsters may possess attributes from at least two of the groups. Although further refinements of their labels may not be possible given how complex each of us is, the work of Chess and Thomas still has major implications for parents and teachers. In highlighting the differences among children from birth, we are reminded of something that seems so obvious, but something that we must continue to reflect upon: different approaches will be required to reach and teach different children.

There is always a danger of pigeonholing children into categories, but I think it would be helpful to look at the three kinds of children mentioned by Chess and Thomas. *Easy children* are rather delightful to raise. From birth they seem to say to their parents, "We're going to make you feel like the best parents in the world." When they begin school they seem to communicate the same message to their teachers. As easy children develop, parents never hesitate taking them places, knowing that they will behave appropriately. Parents of easy children look forward to school conferences (and teachers look forward to having such conferences), anticipating all of the positive things that they will hear. These parents also look forward to Little League games, soccer games, basketball games, and concerts at school, because they know that their children will excel. Easy children help us feel like good parents and good teachers.

Slow-to-warm-up children, as the name implies, need additional time to acclimate to many new situations. Their behavior often prompts people to describe them as shy, timid, or anxious, although these may not be accurate labels. Rather, their innate temperament requires more time to become accustomed to new experiences and new people than does that of some of their peers.

Difficult children are very challenging to raise and to educate. They typically have problems adapting comfortably to new situations. They may demonstrate intense responses and overreactions to many experiences, reveal little pleasure in what they do, appear to be insatiable in their demands, have problems with eating and sleeping, and fail to attend to what others say. It is not easy to relate to many difficult children; they often leave parents and teachers feeling frustrated, angry, and not very competent.

For example, I remember evaluating a six-year-old who easily fit the difficult child category. In my office he tried to open every drawer, even one that was locked. Given his activity level and his impulsivity, he knocked things over, ran from one activity to the next so that I had little opportunity to engage him, wanted to take home almost every toy and game I had in my office, and became annoyed when I told him he could not. I recall how exhausted this child made me feel, and although I am not proud to admit it, I kept looking at my watch and thinking about when the session would finally be over. Obviously, he did not help me feel like a very effective psychologist.

When the session ended and I brought him back to the waiting room, I couldn't help but notice how exhausted his mother appeared. (Perhaps some projection on my part was operating.) In a subsequent session with his parents, his mother poignantly revealed how she had felt like the most inadequate mother in the world from the moment she first held him and he attempted to squirm out of her arms.

It is evident that some children will be much more challenging to parents and teachers than will other children. In so many ways, having a difficult child at home or in our classroom will frequently require an inordinate amount of effort and the results may not always reflect the energy we expend. Love, caring, and patience may not lead, at least at first, to the warm, positive relationships for which we hope or to the development of a child with high self-esteem. When parents tell me that they hesitate to take their difficult child to a restaurant (even a fast-food restaurant), supermarket, department store, or a friend's house for fear of how their child will behave, I can readily grasp what an impact a difficult child can have on a family's life. However, it is important to remember that while certain temperamental characteristics define the difficult child, some parents or teachers may not experience a so-called difficult child as very difficult to relate to or manage. Not surprisingly, our own temperamental styles, goals, and expectations greatly influence our perception of and reaction to each child's unique style. This brings us to the other major factor involved in the formation of a child's self-esteem—the responses to and impact of the environment.

Interactions With the Environment

I recall being somewhat surprised during my initial period of training by my different reactions to patients. I eagerly looked forward to seeing some, while I was not as enthused about seeing others. How naive I had been to assume that I would feel the same way about all of my patients! For example, I remember that I felt more comfortable with children and adolescents who readily showed their anger in words and actions than I did with youngsters whose behavior was more passive-aggressive. I sensed I knew where I stood with the first group and could respond accordingly, while I felt more at a loss and frustrated with patients who communicated their feelings less directly. With further training, I learned how vital it was to become aware of my different reactions to patients so that I could more effectively accommodate my style to theirs in order to form a positive relationship.

My experiences as a therapist are not unlike those encountered by teachers and parents, in that each of us finds some children easier to relate to than others. As an obvious example, parents with an active, gregarious style may encounter more stress and tension raising a child who tends to be cautious and reserved than they would if their child's style was more in keeping with their own. Or parents who were painfully shy as children may be especially upset and angry if they see the same characteristics in their own child. Rather than being understanding, they may angrily insist that their child go outside and make friends. Similar tension might exist when very achievement-oriented parents have a child who has trouble paying attention and being organized. They might accuse their child of being lazy and unmotivated, when in fact their child is actually trying very hard but lacks certain cognitive skills to be more successful in learning.

These kinds of "mismatches" between parents and children arouse much anger and disappointment. Children may begin to feel that they have let their parents down and that they are failures. Low self-esteem is a common result, unless parents are able to modify their goals, expectations, and responses in a direction that is more in step with their child's style.

If we now turn to teachers, we can see the potential for mismatches in the classroom as well. While some students obviously will evoke the same feelings—whether positive or negative—in almost all educators, I have also observed situations in which a teacher's own temperament and style can influence how a particular student is viewed. I recall a boy I worked with who could be somewhat oppositional and demanding. His third-grade teacher, whose style was rather structured and not very flexible, frequently locked horns with this child and saw him as disrespectful and not interested in learning. In contrast, his fourth-grade teacher's flexibility, as demonstrated by different choices and responsibilities she provided her class, lessened my patient's defiance and heightened his cooperation. Even difficult children may not manifest problematic behaviors in a classroom that respects and works *with* rather than against their style and interests.

A Dynamic, Ongoing Interaction

In essence, the development of self-esteem involves a very complex, dynamic, ongoing interaction between individuals and their environment. The unique qualities of children—including those qualities that are inborn—will not only influence how others respond to them but also how they perceive the responses of others. (Some children, for example, seem more predisposed to seeing the actions of others in a positive way, while other youngsters are more prone to experience what others say and do as critical, judgmental, or inconsiderate.) These perceptions will then play a role in determining the subsequent reactions of children, which in turn will elicit particular reactions from the environment.

To illustrate this interactive cycle, think first about children who are easily comforted and satisfied. When we encounter these children, it is likely that, even without realizing it, we will want to spend more time with them—and that the time we spend will be more rewarding. In contrast, if certain children, such as those with a so-called difficult temperament, perceive our caregiving or teaching efforts as not very satisfying, it would not be surprising to find ourselves communicating our annoyance and frustration, in subtle or not-so-subtle ways. Such negative messages would serve only to reinforce the child's perception that the world is not very giving, and the child would respond accordingly.

Given this complicated picture of child-environment interactions, if we are to reinforce a child's self-esteem, it is essential that we attempt to recognize and respond to the unique qualities of each child. As Stanley Coopersmith has so vividly noted, one of the most important components of fostering a positive self-image in children is to accept them for who they are and not for what we want them to be, that is, to accept and respect their individuality. Coopersmith observes:

> Such acceptance does not mean that the parent or teacher approves of all the child's qualities, but it does mean that the teacher or parent can see the child for what he is without being confused by his own feelings of dissatisfaction and desire to change him. . . . Without such acceptance he cannot be viewed for his strengths as well as limitations. Without such acceptance he can be ignored readily and rejected until he totally complies. Without such acceptance the child does not have the emotional support to change and try new ways of behaving.[3]

Accepting children for who they are is easier said than

done. We all have our likes and dislikes, our strengths and blind spots. However, if we are to foster the self-esteem of students, we must become increasingly aware of our own blind spots, lest we fail to recognize the islands of competence of those we are educating. As Robert Rosenthal has found, the expectations teachers have of students play an important role in determining how well students perform in the classroom.[4] The freer we are from our own prejudices to appreciate and respond positively to each child's individuality—even toward those children who are most frustrating, challenging, and difficult to reach—the closer we are to being a self-esteem teacher.

Our Own Self-Esteem

Before turning to specific strategies that can be used in the classroom to reinforce students' self-esteem, I want to address a question that is frequently raised at my workshops. On many occasions teachers have asked me if they can strengthen the self-esteem of students if they themselves are struggling with a negative self-image. They wonder if they do not feel very competent or if they do not perceive their work as important, will they communicate their self-doubts to their students and lessen their effectiveness as teachers?

I believe that a teacher's self-esteem is a significant variable in determining the kind of environment that is established in a classroom. Teachers who lack confidence are more inclined to focus on the negative rather than the positive attributes of students, are less likely to convey an excitement about teaching and learning. Given their insecurities, these teachers are more vulnerable to becoming involved in power struggles and issues of control with their students. The magic that can exist in a classroom will be overwhelmed by boredom, indifference, or defiance.

But what steps can teachers take to strengthen their own sense of self-worth? It is never an easy task to enhance one's own self-esteem, especially if we have to battle negative self-feelings that have existed for years. A first step is to become increasingly aware of how we view ourselves, both our strengths and vulnerabilities. For instance, if we were asked to describe ourselves, what words would we use? If we were asked what we liked about ourselves and what we would want to change, how would we respond?

Another step is never to lose sight of the very significant role that teachers play in children's lives and how our self-image impacts on our teaching. A teacher once told me that when people he met outside of the school asked what he did, he responded, "I'm just a teacher." Once he realized how demeaning his response was, he could take some action to change.

Although we may never understand all of the variables that contribute positively or negatively to our self-esteem, once we appreciate how our self-confidence influences our relationship with our students and our ability to teach, we can begin to take action to strengthen our self-esteem. We can articulate more clearly what our own islands of competence are and then use these islands in our teaching. We can reflect upon what it is that frustrates and angers us and then make a concerted effort to deal more effectively with the feelings and situations that are counterproductive to teaching and to developing warm relationships with our students. We can set more realistic and achievable goals for ourselves and our students and begin to initiate changes not only in our classroom, but when possible, in the overall structure and climate of the school.

This task of self-reflection and change is difficult and challenging. Yet, given the alternative of continued self-doubt and the possibility of a negative classroom environment, it is a challenge well worth facing. The self-esteem strategies that I will now describe will be most effective when designed and implemented by teachers who believe that they can truly make a difference in a child's life.

Chapter Six

SELF-ESTEEM STRATEGIES: A FEW PRELIMINARY REMARKS

"I remember a college professor who taught with humor and enthusiasm. He loved what he did. It always made the course a joy to participate in because he truly loved what he did. That course made me choose my profession. I remember him with such warmth and pleasure."

I should like to make a few points before we examine specific strategies you can use in your classroom and school to foster the self-esteem of students. Right from the start, I want to emphasize that I would not be surprised to find you are already doing many of the things that will be suggested; also, you will probably be able to think of strategies and examples that I have not even mentioned. I want to encourage you to continue to develop your own strategies and in the process to enlarge your capacity to be a self-esteem teacher.

My intention in writing this book is not to come across as a so-called expert here to tell you how to do your job. As a matter of fact, I believe that if experts ever come to your school to tell you how to teach, you should first ask them to work side by side with you for a year so that they can get to know you, the students you teach, the culture of the school, and the neighborhood—only then they can make recommendations. I know that I would not be very receptive if an expert visited the hospital in which I work and told me how I should conduct therapy without knowing more about me, my therapeutic style, and the patients I see.

The objective of the *Seeds of Self-Esteem* approach is to offer ideas and strategies for fostering the self-worth of students—ideas and strategies that are drawn from experiences with many educators and school systems. While I will provide examples of each strategy for illustration purposes, as you become increasingly aware of the principles upon which the strategies are based, you will be able to generate and implement your own strategies given the needs of your students and your own particular interests and teaching style. One of the numerous benefits I have gained from offering workshops in many school systems is hearing firsthand about the creative and powerful interventions that have been developed by teachers to promote the self-esteem of their students.

To Be Knowledgeable and Excited

We must remember that a basic purpose of using self-esteem strategies in the school setting is to help students develop a feeling of pride and enjoyment for learning. Self-esteem will be heightened as students develop the skills to deal with life's challenges. Obviously, the competence of teachers in the subject matter they are teaching is a fundamental variable in the learning process. Such educators serve as models in demonstrating the joy and significance of being informed and competent. It may be very evident, but we should always remind ourselves that the self-esteem strategies discussed in this book will be most effective when used by teachers who are knowledgeable about and take pride in what they are teaching.

Strategies of Broad Applicability

It is important to emphasize the broad applicability of the strategies that I will describe in the following chapters.

These self-esteem strategies are not limited to a particular
group of students. I have seen their impact on children of all
ages and in all grades. The strategies can and should be used
with every student regardless of ethnic, racial, or
socioeconomic background. A child's background and
interests should serve as sources of information in
determining the specific form of the strategy that will have
the greatest probability for success—not whether these
strategies should be used at all. Also, the strategies can be
designed to be used with one student or a group of students.

I have sometimes been asked if self-esteem strategies are
especially relevant and necessary for children with
behavioral or learning problems. While the self-worth of
these children is frequently less secure and in greater need
of reinforcement than that of children not beset with such
problems, all children will benefit from a focus on fostering
self-esteem in the classroom.

It is a myth to assume that children with positive
self-images do not require the ongoing use of self-esteem
strategies. Even a child who possesses self-assurance and a
strong motivation to learn can be adversely affected by a
classroom environment that is not very supportive or
encouraging. This adverse reaction will most likely be more
pronounced in children who are already feeling the burden
of self-doubt and a lack of confidence.

Strategies Without Financial Costs

Another point I wish to emphasize, which will become
apparent as you read the examples, is that the design and
implementation of these strategies need not require any
financial costs—an important factor, given the shrinking
budgets available to most schools. Our creativity, sensitivity,
and caring are the finances that support these strategies.
The potential dividends from that investment are in many
ways limitless. Also, you will see that these strategies may
overlap at times so that many of the interventions you use to
foster self-esteem will rely upon components from two or
more strategies. I believe that the simultaneous use of

different self-esteem strategies will increase the effectiveness of your intervention.

On a number of occasions, educators at my workshops have told me in a complimentary manner that the strategies I described are "just good common sense." I am encouraged by this kind of remark since our actions to promote self-esteem *should* make sense. If anything, it is my hope that as you read about these strategies they will resonate with your own thoughts, efforts, and practices, that they will not seem alien to how you think or what you do as a teacher. It is my hope that you will like and appreciate these strategies because their use does make sense and because they have housed within them the potential for significant benefits to you and your students.

A Partnership With Parents

Although this book focuses primarily on your relationship with students and the impact you can have on fostering their self-esteem, we should not lose sight of the importance of involving parents in this task. Increasing evidence shows that parent-teacher cooperation and parental involvement in the educational process are influential forces in creating more effective schools.[1] A Massachusetts Department of Education report, titled *Educating the Whole Student: The School's Role in the Physical, Intellectual, Social and Emotional Development of Children*, noted:

> Since both the parent and the school are concerned about the child, their continued cooperation and communication are vital in helping children develop the cognitive and affective skills necessary to achieve academic success. Research has shown that this cooperative effort succeeds when the school environment is welcoming to parents and encouraging of their participation and input. Although the reality of two parents working and the single parent family makes these tasks difficult, there are ways for schools to involve parents.[2]

Zelma Solomon has voiced similar thoughts about parent-school relationships:

Any school can be more successful if parents are
productively involved in their children's education. Any
student can be more successful if schools link comprehensive
parent involvement programs to curricula and to teaching and
learning.[3]

Programs in schools will be all the more successful if a
concerted effort is made to engage and work collaboratively
with parents. As Joyce Epstein has noted, a solid working
relationship between parents and schools can be realized in
various ways such as assisting parents to develop more
effective parenting skills; informing parents of techniques
they can use at home to help their children learn; fostering
close two-way communication with parents; involving
parents, after necessary training, in providing instruction
and support in the school setting; involving parents in the
decision-making process of schools so that they can truly
participate in how the schools are governed.[4]

The *Seeds of Self-Esteem* approach will be most effective
when teachers and parents work cooperatively in articulating
and refining realistic goals and strategies for fostering
self-esteem. At the beginning of the year, perhaps at an open
school night, through written communication, or by means of
both, you can share your views with parents about the
importance of self-esteem in all facets of their children's
lives. You might also describe techniques that will be used in
school to reinforce their children's self-esteem. You can
emphasize that strategies used in school can be
complemented by similar strategies used at home. You can
encourage parents' feedback and welcome an ongoing
dialogue about the rationale and form of self-esteem
interventions, emphasizing the significant role that parents
play in reinforcing a positive self-image in children.

The open, respectful dialogue that you nurture with
parents throughout the school year will serve as a source of
energy to strengthen the strategies you use and propel you
toward your goals as a self-esteem teacher.

Chapter Seven

TO ESTABLISH AN ALLIANCE: CREATING A SENSE OF IDENTITY AND BELONGING

"In the fourth and fifth grades, the school librarian used to spend time picking out books with me and always put aside the new books which she thought I would like. It made me feel important and that someone valued my interests."

"My second-grade teacher wrote a personal note to me after I was in her class."

"My fourth-grade teacher always asked if I would help with the bulletin boards. She thought that I was artistic. Whenever I helped her, she always talked to me about things other than school. It made me feel like a real person, not just a student."

"In the third grade, my teacher had conferences with my parents with me there and would tell wonderful stories about me and the schoolwork I did."

Perhaps the most influential force in determining the effectiveness of self-esteem strategies is the relationship that students have with their teachers and among themselves. Although the use of any of the strategies highlighted in this book will serve to strengthen these relationships, I believe we should give special attention at the beginning of the school year to developing an *alliance* with students. The concept of alliance is typically used in discussions of the psychotherapeutic process, but it has equal applicability to the relationship we have with students and the relationship we help students develop with each other.

The presence of an alliance in a classroom implies trust and cooperation between teacher and student and among the students. It is reflected in students' feeling a sense of security and belonging, a comfort in knowing that they can reveal their vulnerabilities, that they can take risks, that they will not be demeaned or judged or accused, that they will be supported and encouraged for their efforts, and that their individuality will be respected and accepted. An alliance provides the fertile soil in which self-esteem strategies can bear their greatest fruit. In turn, the strategies provide further nutriments to this rich soil.

Given the central role that teacher-student and student-student relationships play in fostering self-esteem, I plan in this chapter to focus on specific attitudes and strategies that can serve to nurture these alliances from the beginning of the school year. This goal of nurturing the alliance should not be confined only to the first few weeks of school, but rather needs to be present throughout the year, finding expression in all that we say and do in the classroom.

To Appreciate Each Student's Individuality

How do we help all students feel that they are unique individuals who are welcome and belong in our classroom? As I mentioned earlier in this book, a first step is to try to remember what it was like when we were youngsters. Which teachers helped us to feel we were respected and were an important part of their classroom? What did they do to make us feel this way? In contrast, which teachers acted in ways that worked against developing an alliance with us, and what did they do to create such a negative climate? We can use our own indelible memories of school to guide what we do today with students.

I believe that to help students feel they belong is a basic task of the self-esteem teacher. It is a responsibility that will reinforce the development of an alliance.[1] In accomplishing this task, we must learn to understand and accept the uniqueness of each student—a much greater challenge than we often realize. In creating our classroom climate and expectations, we should consider the individual differences among students. We must recognize that each student enters school with different strengths and vulnerabilities, that each student's style of learning and taking in information differs, and that each student relies upon different strategies to cope with the demands of learning and school.

I want to emphasize that responding to the individuality of each student does not mean that you will have to develop a separate lesson plan for each, especially since there are many commonalities among students in any classroom. What I am suggesting is that an alliance with students will be enhanced if the structure and expectations of our classrooms permit the individual style of each student to shine. I recall a teacher—working closely with the principal—who ensured that the more active children in her classroom had outlets for their activity by creating different responsibilities that respected and actually utilized their style. For instance, one especially active boy was often recruited to be the class messenger to bring notes to the main office. Another boy, who needed time at the beginning of each school day to settle in, became the "attendance monitor," walking down the hall with a clipboard given to him each morning by the school principal. The clipboard held a sheet with all of the room numbers listed; the principal told the boy that it would help if he would look into each room from the hallway to see if a teacher was present and to inform the principal if any classroom did not have a teacher. This responsibility helped to acclimate this very active boy to the school environment each morning, making it easier for him to adjust to the requirements of the school day. I continue to be impressed by the strategies educators use that accept and respect rather than oppose a child's basic style and temperament.

To Create a Sense of Being Special and Belonging

In forming an alliance, we can strive to help each student and class feel special since students are more likely to learn and less likely to rebel if they possess this feeling. To help students feel special does not imply that we are reinforcing conceit or narcissism, but rather self-respect and belonging. As educators, we have to ask ourselves if we have made the effort to get to know each student, if we have truly listened to what each one is saying. I realize that with twenty-five or more students in a class, teachers are not able to spend a great deal of individualized time, but even with time limitations, we have ways to communicate to students that we believe they are important and that we care about them. This may be accomplished by seemingly small gestures—a smile or learning each student's name quickly. I remember evaluations I received at the end of the semester when I was teaching three college classes, each with about thirty students; it was interesting that a number of students commented in a very positive way that I had made the effort to learn each student's name as early as possible in the school year.

I am reminded of one elementary school teacher who called each child and each parent in her class the day before school began to welcome the children and to let the parents know that they could contact her should any questions arise. This teacher told me that the calls, which served to convey to students and parents that she cared about them, took less time than she had originally anticipated. She said that the calls were well worth the effort, given the positive climate this initial contact helped establish. Relatedly, a kindergarten teacher, who was to have one of my patients in her class, sent a postcard to each of her incoming students a couple of weeks before school began. (Children love to receive mail.) The parents read the postcard to the students, which said that the teacher was looking forward to having them in her class and invited them to bring in a photo of themselves as well as a picture they had drawn. I am certain my patient's response was representative of his classmates. He was very pleased to have his photo and a picture he had drawn displayed in the classroom on the first day of school. He felt an immediate sense of specialness and belonging.

I have been asked, when I describe these kinds of examples at my workshops, what would happen if a child did not have a photo or neglected to bring in a drawing. It is important always to be prepared for such possible glitches in any strategy we use so that we maximize the probability for success. For instance, if a teacher were to use the strategy of hanging a photo, drawing, or both, and the child did not bring one in, perhaps a Polaroid camera might be available and the child's photo could be taken during the first day of class. Or a related strategy could be used such as reported by a teacher who took a class photo within the first couple of days of school and taped it on the wall. As mentioned in the previous chapter, the particular forms of the strategies you use should be based on your interests, teaching style, and knowledge of the students in your class.

When I was director of a school (called the Psychoeducation Unit) for children and adolescents who were hospitalized in a locked-door unit at the Hall-Mercer Center for Children and Adolescents of McLean Hospital (a psychiatric facility), I struggled with the task of helping our patients feel welcomed in a learning environment that many at first called a "jail" because of its locked doors. In addition to having an initial session with each patient, I also encouraged the scheduling of brief, individual meetings with me throughout the hospitalization. I did this, in part, in response to the frequency with which patients barged into my office even when I was with someone else. I wanted to convey the message that I was available, but I also wanted these youths to learn to respect both my privacy and the privacy of their peers. To accomplish this, I set aside times each day when a student could sign up for five-minute meetings with me. (More time if necessary could also be arranged.) It was impressive to witness how, once these patients saw their names in my appointment book and realized that I would have time for them, they refrained from coming into my office unannounced. They experienced these appointments as special times, reinforcing the feeling that I cared about them.

Creating special times for students is something I believe that all educators can do without much effort since in many respects it is being done already, though often not in a systematic way. Many teachers have told me that they attempt to spend individual time with each student to promote a closer relationship. Interestingly, however, many students may not experience these interactions with their teachers as an expression of being cared for and respected. (This is especially true in those classrooms in which teachers hold individual meetings with students primarily when the students have done something wrong.) To reinforce messages of caring and belonging, I often advocate that, at the beginning of the year, teachers inform students that brief appointment times have been built into the class routine so that teacher and student can get to know each other. The teacher can schedule the initial appointment with each student, and then either the teacher or the student can schedule subsequent meetings.

In response to my recommending these special times, some teachers have voiced concern that their schedules would become even more burdensome. Yet, in feedback I have received, teachers often report that the inclusion of these brief appointments does not add time to their day; if anything, they feel that for many students—especially those in the lower grades—the meetings foster a sense of security and attachment and lessen overly dependent behavior. Scheduled appointments and the spontaneous interactions that take place throughout the school day are not mutually exclusive. Rather, the appointments complement these interactions and serve as a concrete way to highlight a teacher's availability—a powerful vehicle through which teachers can listen actively and respond effectively to what their students are communicating. Related to this last point, teachers have told me that students learn to respect and not interrupt the appointment times of their classmates, allowing the teacher to be less distracted, more focused, and more empathic when engaged in an appointment with a student.

To Create a Classroom Identity

In addition to strategies that help each student feel valued and special, there are strategies that can be used specifically to foster the alliance among students, to create a classroom identity, a sense of cohesiveness in which students truly feel that they belong to a group. For instance, if you asked most students the name of their class, they would probably look confused or respond with such general labels as "third grade," "fifth grade," "Mrs. Jones," "Mr. Smith," "social studies," "math." Might not many students enjoy giving their class a nickname or label that would serve to define the identity of the group? Perhaps the students could even design a class emblem that would appear on the door leading into the room. Also, a class diary could be kept, in which students took turns at the end of the day recording events that had occurred in the class or school (for example, when the class sang at an assembly or decorated the hallway) or even outside the school (such as an account of a game played by a town or city sports team or a significant world event such as the launching of a space shuttle). The diary could also include the birthdays of the children and important happenings in their lives (for example, the birth of a sibling). At the end of the year, the teacher might even like to make copies of the diary so that all of the students would have their own history of the class.

I remember supervising two psychologists who were conducting therapy with a group of young adolescent girls. The first couple of sessions were characterized by the teens' disruptiveness and lack of cooperation. In hearing what was occurring, I felt that there was an absence of a group purpose and identity and that the girls felt little, if any, responsibility for what transpired in the meetings. I discussed these thoughts with the therapists. In the next session, they presented the girls with choices of different responsibilities, including the naming of the group, having one of the members inform the others when the group was to begin, having someone alert the group when five minutes remained in the session, and having one of the members record in a diary what had occurred during that session. These tasks had a calming effect on the girls and helped create a group identity and a strong sense of belonging and purpose. It also promoted an alliance with the therapists.

There are many tasks we can offer our students that will bring them together as a group and reinforce their self-esteem. Organizing and running a charity drive[2] and being involved in cooperative learning activities[3] are but two examples. Jeanne Gibbs vividly captured the power of cooperative groups in her description of the Tribes program,[4] noting that the creation of long-term, supportive classroom groups improved students' self-esteem, enhanced respect for teachers, decreased behavior problems, and increased motivation to learn. We have much to gain by fostering an alliance among our students, by nurturing a group purpose and a group identity. Subsequent chapters in this book will include further consideration of the group alliance.

If we are to create classroom environments conducive to the development of self-esteem, we must sharpen our skills in developing an alliance, in respecting the individuality of each student, and in promoting a feeling of belonging among all students. In addition, we must learn to understand, appreciate, and "join" the coping strategies of our students. It is to the important topic of the relationship between alliance-building and coping strategies that we now turn.

Chapter Eight

TO ESTABLISH AN ALLIANCE: UNDERSTANDING, RESPECTING, AND "JOINING" THE COPING STRATEGIES OF OUR STUDENTS

"When presenting an oral book report—a difficult personal task—my teacher allowed those of us who preferred sitting to do so. It was a positive experience and opened the door for me!"

"I was sneaking pistachio nuts in Spanish class. The teacher came over to me, and, instead of ridiculing me, he showed me how to open them so my fingers wouldn't hurt! Then he ate some himself!"

The ways in which children cope with challenges and pressures are considered in the design and implementation of all the self-esteem strategies described in this book and will be especially addressed in the chapter dealing with discipline. However, I believe that unless we understand more clearly the purposes that coping strategies serve and the different forms in which they find expression, we will encounter major barriers in our attempts to develop an alliance with students. For this reason, I decided to devote a separate chapter to the topic of coping strategies and their relationship to building an alliance.

What Are Coping Strategies?

What is meant by *coping strategies*? If I were to ask you to think about a coping strategy that you used and a time that you used it, what example would come to mind? As you think about that example, think about what purpose your coping behavior served and how helpful it was. We all use different means to cope throughout our lives as we deal with a multitude of challenges, stresses, and pressures. Some techniques for coping are more adaptive and in the service of growth, while other techniques keep us from realizing our potential. For instance, have you ever been asked to make a presentation to a professional or community group? We all know that giving a talk can be very anxiety provoking, placing us in a position of feeling exposed and vulnerable to possible embarrassment and humiliation should we make mistakes. When invited to make a presentation, some individuals quickly say no, offering different reasons for their reply. ("There are people who know more about this topic than I do. I hate to speak in public. I won't have enough time to prepare.") Others say yes. Even upon saying yes, people cope differently: Some will do hours of research on the topic while others will not; some will read their speech verbatim while others will follow an outline.

I remember being asked to present a talk to a community group about stress in children. To break the ice at the start of my talk as well as to illustrate a point about stress, I asked for a volunteer to take a test dealing with conceptual thinking that I said was related to the evening's topic. It was interesting and not surprising to see how almost everyone coped—the same way that many of us coped when we were in school and did not want the teacher to call on us. People stopped looking at me and glanced down; it was as if by not facing me they were hopeful I would not call on them. Finally, the woman who had invited me to speak, perhaps prompted by some sense of obligation, volunteered to take the test. With some humor, I shared with the audience what I had just observed. We talked about the pressure we feel when we are asked to respond or perform in public, something that occurs almost every day for our children. We also discussed the ways we cope with this pressure.

Before examining more closely the function of coping strategies, let's look at what we have observed with our students. If I were to ask you to describe different forms of coping that you have witnessed your students use, what examples would come to mind? I am certain that some of the examples would represent adaptive attempts at coping such as a student who was having difficulty with long division asking for extra help, or a child with poor peer relationships making an effort not to put down classmates. However, often the coping behaviors of our students that we recall most vividly are those that would not be considered very adaptive, effective, or appropriate. Not only have teachers provided me with numerous examples of such counterproductive forms of coping, but I have witnessed many firsthand both when I directed the Psychoeducation Unit at McLean Hospital and in my therapy sessions.

The following are but a few illustrations:

• A child who failed a math test and blamed the teacher for supposedly including items on the test that the child claimed had not been covered in class.

• A child who was being teased, and sought refuge by constantly going to the bathroom.

• A child who played the part of the class clown, always joking around and minimizing learning problems.

• A child who scapegoated and bullied other students.

• A child who fell asleep in the classroom (I remember when this happened to one of my patients in a one-to-one therapy session with me—and I thought that I was an exciting therapist!).

• A child who desperately attempted to please everyone, never showing any anger.

• An adolescent who during our first therapy session called me the "ugliest shrink" he had ever seen (What an insult! But I relied on my own coping strategy by rationalizing that he had seen only two other shrinks in his life so that the sample with whom I was being compared was not very large.).

• A child who ran out of my office when I attempted to talk with him about problems he was experiencing.

• A child who agreed to complete her homework, but seldom did, offering all kinds of excuses.

As teachers and therapists, we're only human. When we reach out to help youngsters and they cope by rejecting or sabotaging our efforts, we are likely to become annoyed and angry; we cannot easily hide these feelings, feelings that unfortunately lessen our effectiveness. All of us can think about an occasion when we experienced some relief upon learning that a certain student was out sick and we would not see that individual on that day. This sense of relief is typically a sign of our frustration and helplessness in not knowing how to reach or work with the child or adolescent in question. Our frustration and subsequent anger become obstacles to developing or maintaining an alliance.

To remove these obstacles, we must struggle to understand the behaviors of our students. We need to ask ourselves, "What purpose do coping strategies serve? What are our students coping with? How can we best respond to coping behaviors shown by our students that are self-defeating and disruptive, and that interfere with learning?" These are questions that deserve serious consideration. In attempting to offer an answer, I will share some thoughts about coping behaviors that have helped guide my work and make my efforts more effective.

Coping Strategies: To Maintain Dignity and Self-Esteem

I constantly remind myself that one of the main reasons we use coping strategies is to attempt to maintain a sense of dignity and self-esteem. Unfortunately, some of the ways we cope may actually serve to lessen our self-worth. To use an earlier example, when we turn down a request to give a talk, it is usually because of our fears of doing a poor job and feeling embarrassed. We say no in order not to face a situation that might lower our self-esteem. The relief we experience by saying no is often temporary at best, replaced by anger at ourselves for not trying. However, when we later receive a similar request to make a presentation, we frequently say no again, still fearful of failing. The erosion of our self-esteem continues.

Turning our attention to students, those who blame the teacher for a poor test grade or become the class clown or scream "I don't care" when confronted with evidence of their not doing homework are students who are struggling to hide any sign of weakness. They expend a great deal of energy fleeing from challenging tasks and from their mistakes and failures. They run to avoid what they perceive to be possibilities for further humiliation and embarrassment since they entertain little hope of succeeding. They are motivated by the belief that avoiding a challenge is better than confronting it and failing. Their coping maneuvers, although ultimately ineffective and counterproductive, are the equivalent of a shield of armor, protecting the vulnerabilities and low self-esteem that engulf their lives.

Yet, it is interesting to observe the ways in which many of us respond to the coping behaviors of our students. As a consequence of our frustration and anger, our ability to be empathic is lessened. We often demand that our students remove their protective shields before they have learned to trust us and before an alliance has been established; in response, they will put on an even stronger piece of armor.

A Change of Focus: Don't Blame the Children

As I became more aware of the function that coping strategies played, I altered my approach. I recognized that subtly, or perhaps not so subtly, I had been placing all of the blame on students and patients for their counterproductive coping behaviors. I was quick to label these youngsters "resistant," never entertaining the thought that their teachers or I might bear some responsibility for triggering or reinforcing the resistant behavior. I assumed that if students did not want to do their homework or patients did not want to listen to what I had to say, it was their problem—my job was to devise techniques for totally eradicating these strategies of avoidance and resistance. My assumptions and goals changed when I came to appreciate that even those coping behaviors that turned out to be self-defeating were initially recruited by children or adolescents to maintain self-esteem and protection in an environment they perceived to be threatening.

With this new perspective, I shifted my focus from casting blame to searching for ways to do two things: First, I sought to create learning and therapeutic environments that would maximize success experiences and be less threatening to children so that they would not have to rely so desperately on their protective shields—in essence, to develop in students a respectable level of competence in all subjects, but especially those that had proven problematic for them in the past. Second, I learned to take risks, to "join" and modify students' self-defeating strategies rather than try to strip them away.

I adopted the position that when children and adolescents become so-called disciplinary problems and when they rely on coping strategies that serve primarily to avoid challenges, our responsibility is to examine the ways in which our teaching or therapeutic style might be contributing to the use of these strategies. I am not suggesting that we are to blame for the counter-productive maneuvers, discipline problems, or lack of motivation of our students or that we should passively accept the presence of these behaviors. What I am advocating is that we assume responsibility for designing learning environments that develop competencies in academic areas, minimize the fear of failure, highlight the islands of strength of our students, and hold our students responsible and accountable for their actions—but in a manner that is not perceived by them as demeaning, controlling, or judgmental.

Other clinicians and educators have also advanced the view that in forming an alliance, we must not be derailed by some of the disruptive coping behaviors of our students, but must understand what these behaviors represent. As Howard Adelman and Linda Taylor, drawing upon the work of

Edward Deci and his colleagues, emphasized, all individuals have a need for self-determination, competence, and belonging. When these needs are thwarted, for example, by an environment that students experience as overly controlling, rigid, or punitive, we will likely witness reactions on their part that will be classified as disruptive or oppositional.[1]

As will become apparent in the following chapters, all of the self-esteem strategies outlined in this book strive to reinforce a sense of self-determination, self-control, autonomy, competence, and belonging. If these strategies to reinforce self-esteem are used effectively, they will minimize the need for students to rely on coping behaviors that interfere with the development of a productive, secure classroom environment.

There will always be students, however, who will test our patience, who will enter our classrooms with both a temperamental style and a history that make them very vulnerable to engaging in disruptive behavior. They are students who often experience class rules as instruments to control them and limit their freedom; they perceive efforts to correct their work and help them learn as attempts to locate their Achilles' heel. They are trapped in what I call a "negative script," unable to see or respond to others in a more positive way. Their reactions have a knee-jerk, predictable quality as they push us away and reject our help. It is often a Herculean task to develop an alliance with them.

To Take Risks and Change Negative Scripts

How can we change the negative scripts of students, enabling us to foster a positive relationship with them that will promote learning and success in the classroom? I believe we must be willing to take risks and change our typical response to these students. We must be willing to alter our own predictable scripts. For example, in the last chapter I told of a very active boy whose behavior was disruptive to the class. Frequently, our response to such a child is to remind him to sit in his seat, perhaps even to punish him for failing to do so. Instead, in this instance the teacher and principal changed the script by enlisting him in the role of an attendance monitor, a position that respected his temperament and coping style; his disruptive ways of coping decreased noticeably.

I was seeing a sixth-grade girl in therapy who was referred to me because of oppositional behavior. She often failed to do her homework, claiming that the assignments were too easy or that she had forgotten to bring her books home. I met with her teacher, who understandably was feeling quite frustrated by this girl's lack of cooperation. We discussed the possible sources of this noncompliant behavior. My patient appeared to feel very incompetent and attempted to hide her feelings of inadequacy behind an "I don't care," belligerent attitude.

The approach her teacher and I adopted with the approval of her parents involved changing the script. We learned from the parents that this girl enjoyed interacting with and instructing younger children; we decided to use this seeming island of competence as a starting point in our intervention. Instead of following the more predictable script of insisting in some fashion that she complete all of her homework assignments, we engaged her as a tutor for first and second graders. This strategy was guided by the belief that teaching younger children would help this girl feel more self-assured in the school setting and more willing to face those situations and tasks that made her anxious. Interestingly, when she encountered a younger child who showed some of the same ways of coping that she did (for example, a younger child who could not tolerate making mistakes, would blame my patient for not teaching her correctly and would sometimes say she didn't want to do the work), the encounter served as an opportunity for both the teacher and me to talk with my patient about how this younger child might feel, why some children might resist doing their work, and how she might help this younger child feel more secure and willing to learn. These discussions about the younger student helped my patient acknowledge and confront her own vulnerabilities. As a consequence, my patient's self-esteem and productivity improved.

An example of changing the script and joining rather than opposing a student's coping strategy occurred when I was director of the Psychoeducation Unit. I encountered a boy whose primary way of coping was to be suspicious and mistrustful. A paranoid flavor was very apparent, especially when he searched my office to make certain there were no hidden microphones before he would talk with me. He refused to go into his classroom, contending that he hated teachers and that they were out to get him. Rather than attempt to convince this boy that he should not be mistrustful—since he did not have an alliance with me, if I had told him that the teachers were not out to get him, he would have felt that I was in partnership with them and would have rejected my efforts—I decided to call upon his suspiciousness as a strategy for helping him enter the classroom and meet his teachers.

I "confessed" that perhaps I did not know as much about my staff as I should and that it would be helpful to learn more about them. I wondered if he would be willing to assist me by becoming the investigative reporter of the school and interviewing each member of the staff. He showed immediate interest and accepted the assignment. We devised questions he might ask such as "Why do you want to teach kids like us who are in a hospital?" and "How do you help kids learn to trust you?" He met individually with the staff members and wrote a newsletter containing our questions and the staff's answers. By accepting and using his main style of coping, I had found a vehicle through which he could develop an alliance with his teachers; in addition, the act of creating a newsletter that was available for the other patients to read not only reinforced academic skills but also helped him feel more a part of the group.

My recommendations for changing the script have met, on occasion, with some resistance on the part of educators. A teacher once accused me of giving in to a child and told me that my approach would lead to a "spoiled child" who would never learn to meet his responsibilities. Actually, I do not view changing the script as giving in to children. If anything, one of my goals in changing scripts is to encourage children and adolescents to become more accountable and responsible for their actions, rather than continuing to adhere rigidly to their self-defeating patterns of behavior. Changing scripts need not suggest the absence of expectations, rules, and consequences.

I believe that in order to motivate students and help them relinquish disruptive and counterproductive coping behaviors, we must provide them with opportunities that enhance their self-worth so that they can experience the benefits of facing rather than running from challenges, of persevering at tasks in order to enjoy the sense of exhilaration that often accompanies the mastery of new material. At times in providing these opportunities, we must respond in new and totally unexpected ways—even seeming to ignore at first the problematic behavior—since our typical responses will serve only to alienate students further.

Obviously, for teachers to feel comfortable in doing the unpredictable and changing scripts, the support of administrators and parents is crucial. When this support is lacking, teachers may need to take the initiative in encouraging an ongoing dialogue with administrators and parents—a dialogue in which trust can be nurtured, classroom goals and interventions can be discussed, and a more effective partnership reached among teachers, parents, and administrators.

The self-esteem teacher is an individual who understands and respects the coping behaviors of students and accepts responsibility for attempting to minimize and modify those behaviors that are counterproductive to classroom success. In displaying the courage to take risks, to change scripts, to accept responsibility, and to maintain faith even in those children who are most resistant to learning, the self-esteem teacher truly serves as a charismatic model. Students who are fortunate enough to interact and develop an alliance with this kind of teacher will begin to feel more confident in examining and changing their own scripts. They will be able to replace self-defeating coping behaviors that rely on avoidance or denial with behaviors characterized by courage and perseverance. They will begin to experience life as a challenge to confront and master rather than a stress to avoid.

Chapter Nine

TO CREATE
A "PSYCHOLOGICAL SPACE"

"In the fourth grade, the teacher allowed my friend and me to wash the walls in the teachers' room! We thought we were the 'cat's meow'!"

"In the second grade, we were making an undersea mural, and my fish was chosen as one to be drawn on the mural. I was able to stay in at recess and add my fish to the seascape."

Years ago an eight-year-old patient was referred to me because of a marked lack of confidence. His primary mode of coping was to quit at tasks that he found difficult. Upon entering my office for the first time, he noticed a shag rug on the floor and some playthings on the shelves (games, puppets, marking pens, modeling clay). He looked surprised and exclaimed, "You have a shag rug and Play-Doh in the same room?" He then looked at children's drawings I had taped to the wall and said, "You let kids hang pictures on your wall?"

Thinking quickly, I asked what it was like at his house. He proceeded to tell me that he had a shag rug in his room (shag rugs were popular in the 1970s), but he was not allowed to use Play-Doh since his parents said it could leave a mess in the rug. He also informed me that he was not permitted to place pictures or posters on the wall since his parents said the tape or tacks that were used would leave marks. His parents were actually caring people, but overly obsessed about cleanliness.

After our first session ended, I wondered what possible impact there might be on this child of having a room that in many respects he did not truly experience as his own, a room governed by what appeared to be some extreme restrictions. My speculation about this particular patient and his room triggered a more general question: Will children develop a greater sense of security, belonging, and responsibility, and will their self-esteem flourish when they are in an environment in which they truly feel that the space is theirs? If the answer was yes, then a related question would be: What can we do to help children feel that the space they inhabit is theirs, that it is their "psychological space"? I was to discover that answers to these questions resided within my own personal experiences as well as in research findings. I was also to discover the importance of developing psychological space as a self-esteem strategy in schools.

Vandalism and the Space Committee

One of the clearest examples for me of the significance of psychological space occurred when the Hall-Mercer Center for Children and Adolescents of McLean Hospital was opened in 1973, and I was asked to be the first director of the Psychoeducation Unit. Very honestly, the staff and I were not prepared for the level of aggression manifested by our patients. Within the first few months, the baseboard radiator system was kicked apart. Obscenities were written on the walls. Wooden chairs were pulled apart. Drawings and posters were ripped down. Overhead lights were broken. Every hour seemed to bring another emergency. The level of frustration and exhaustion was intense, and we resorted to a frenetic crisis intervention style rather than adopting a more thoughtful crisis prevention approach. This period probably represented the lowest point of my professional career—I felt helpless, hopeless, and ineffective.

The vandalism and destruction of property occurred with
such regularity that a Space Committee composed of two
teachers was formed with the task of making a list of the
damage done each week, a list that would be sent over to
Plant and Operations. (Damage that represented immediate
safety issues such as broken glass was reported at once.) I
recall one of the Plant and Operations men saying to me with
a touch of humor, "Bob, just give us ten minutes with these
kids, and your problems will be over." Although I believe he
said this in jest, there were many times I thought that his
implied form of intervention might be more effective than
what we were doing.

One member of the staff raised the possibility of placing
two of the patients on the Space Committee. Another staff
member said that such a step would be the equivalent of
placing an arsonist on the fire department and, if anything, it
might lead to more destruction since it would call even more
attention to the damage taking place. The decision was
finally made, however, to have two patients join the Space
Committee and walk around the Psychoeducation Unit with
the two staff members each week to record damage to the
school environment. Looking back, I recognize that what this
move accomplished was to change the script by empowering
our patients to be more involved in their own treatment
program.

What transpired during the next few weeks was
impressive to behold. The amount of vandalism decreased
noticeably, obscenities were washed from the walls, pictures
and posters went up and stayed up. For the first time, it
seemed that the hospitalized children and adolescents
experienced the Psychoeducation Unit as their space, not as
a jail. Providing them with responsibility for taking care of
the Unit resulted in a physically and psychologically
healthier environment, an environment that was more
conducive to learning and less punctuated with aggressive
behavior.

I should note that eventually the Space Committee was
renamed the Student Committee to reflect the additional

responsibilities being assumed by our patients. However, taking care of the space remains a high priority and interest of the Student Committee. For instance, one of the activities that is monitored by our department's Quality Assurance Committee is the physical condition of the school environment. Four times a day a member of the Student Committee surveys the Psychoeducation Unit to ensure that the environment is safe, and if the student observes any problem (such as furniture being broken or the door to the furnace room being left unlocked), the coordinator of the program is notified and corrective action taken.

As chair of our department's Quality Assurance Committee, I have had the opportunity to talk with the Student Committee about the responsibility of inspecting the school. It is obvious that they perceive this job as very important. It is also apparent that the condition of the environment is intertwined with their behavior, their self-esteem, and their success in the program.

A Memory from the Ninth Grade

This experience at the Psychoeducation Unit elicited a vivid memory from my own school history and helped me gain a clearer understanding of the importance of psychological space. In the ninth grade, I was being bullied by several classmates. I decided that the best way to cope was to avoid school. Since this was certainly not a strategy that would be acceptable to my parents, I made believe I was sick, a performance aided by the use of a thermometer placed for a moment on the radiator. (It is interesting to observe the coping strategies we use when faced with danger.)

For four days, my plan worked. I stayed home and arranged to get the notes from my classes as well as my homework assignments. Then came what I now refer to as "Fateful Friday."

The day began very ominously. I must have kept the thermometer on the radiator for longer than I should have. I still remember my mother standing over my bed, saying in a firm voice, "Bobby, you do not have a fever of one hundred eight. You get to school right now!" Walking to junior high that morning was like walking into the valley of death. I was frightened and confused. Greeting me at the door of the school was Mrs. Roth, who was both my English and homeroom teacher. Mrs. Roth accompanied me to the classroom. As we were going down the hallway she glanced at various signs on the walls (many having to do with rules of the school) and commented that the school looked drab and the signs were in poor condition. (They were all made of oak tag paper.)

Mrs. Roth then asked, "Don't you like to draw signs and posters?" "Yes," I answered, "but how did you know?" "I thought I had heard about that," she responded.

At that moment I should have suspected that she had spoken with my parents, and I should have become even more suspicious a few moments later when we entered the classroom, and I noticed about thirty-five pieces of oak tag paper by her desk. She asked if I might be interested in making new copies of the signs and pointed to the oak tag. I said yes, and she added that I should put my name at the bottom of each sign so others would know that I was responsible for doing them. During the next two weeks I made about thirty-five signs and posters that appeared in all of the hallways. What a feeling to see my work displayed! The school appeared more inviting. The bullies didn't seem as threatening. I no longer thought of playing sick. I even struggled to learn the difference between adverbs and adjectives in Mrs. Roth's English class.

Years later, I realized what Mrs. Roth had done. She had taken one of my islands of competence—drawing signs and posters—and displayed this island throughout the school. She had discovered a strategy to turn a "drab" school into a comfortable psychological space for a student who had been frightened, but who was to become more self-assured.

From Physical Environment to Psychological Space

Given my experiences as a ninth grader and as director of the Psychoeducation Unit, I became increasingly aware of the need to create psychological spaces for our students in order to strengthen their sense of belonging and their self-esteem. My experiences were supported by the research findings of Michael Rutter, a renowned British psychiatrist. Rutter undertook a comprehensive study of British schools, and one of the things he discovered was that displaying the work of students on the walls was associated with greater academic success.[1]

Many teachers intuitively provide activities that transform the school's physical environment into a comfortable psychological space. The teacher mentioned earlier in this book who invited her kindergarten students to bring in a photo and a drawing to be displayed in the classroom helped create such a space on the first day of school. I have visited hundreds of classrooms in preschools, elementary schools, and secondary schools and have been impressed with the student work that is displayed—book reports; abstract art; drawings pertaining to historical figures, ecological themes, characters in books, scientific experiments. These student productions were intertwined with the regular curriculum so that they did not require teachers to find additional time in an already busy schedule. In my visits to schools, it is obvious to me which classrooms and buildings have become warm psychological spaces, conveying the message that students are respected and welcomed and that the school is proud of their accomplishments.

As an example, I recall visiting a middle school that had a painting of a very large tree on one of the walls of the lobby. The "leaves" of the tree were photos of the students. The principal informed me that several of the students who helped paint the tree were young adolescents who were not very motivated about school; she said that producing this tree, which was admired by staff, students, and visitors alike as they entered the building, led to an increased sense of pride and interest in school. Relatedly, I was invited to speak at an elementary school whose lobby was filled with the photos of students, photos taken by the school principal.

What a warm feeling the building had! In another school, I was greeted by plants and drawings that were associated with the science curriculum, and I was told how proud the students were of what they were growing.

I should like to share another example from my past involving my sixth-grade teacher, a man who always made all of the students feel that they belonged in his class. Located a block away from our elementary school was the public library, a facility many of us did not often visit. I recall the day our sixth-grade teacher said that he had shown the head librarian the book reports the class had recently completed. He said that he had asked the librarian if the class could display the reports on one of the walls of the library and the librarian agreed. We all marched over to the library to hang up our reports. I used the library more that year than ever before. The presence of our reports hanging on the walls had transformed the library into our psychological space.

In my clinical work, I am very sensitive to the importance of developing a psychological space in my office. During the first session or two, I typically give my patients a folder and inform them that the folder can be used to hold their drawings and other material. I invite my patients to put their name on the folder and to color the folder if they would like to do so. I also encourage them to place drawings they have done on the office wall. Keeping something of theirs in the office is but one way for me to communicate that the space is theirs.

Examining the Space in Your School

Please think about the techniques you have used to create a psychological space in your classroom and school. Examine your school environment. Have students painted a mural anywhere? Are their reports and drawings displayed? Are they invited to take care of plants? Do they have some input in how their room is arranged?

Also, include the teachers' room in your inspection of the school environment. The condition of this room often reflects the morale and enthusiasm of the staff, attitudes that filter down to the students. I once entered a staff room that had no pictures or posters but did contain a couple of dying plants. What an appearance! I always recommend that the staff room include drawings, cartoons, and works of students. Students might even be enlisted to make decisions about which productions of theirs be included in the teachers' room and then participate in hanging up their work. A staff that respects and is proud of its own space is typically a staff that will assist students to have a similar feeling about the school.

Thus far in discussing psychological space, I have primarily emphasized such activities as displaying the work of students and providing them with responsibilities for taking care of the physical space of the school. Let's look at psychological space through yet another lens, focusing on the physical arrangement of the room. I have observed many different classrooms and have come to realize that the way in which we arrange our room communicates a powerful message about the kinds of relationships and activities we wish to develop. For instance, a room in which students are required to sit in straight rows facing the teacher is one that minimizes interaction among students and in many respects also minimizes student interaction with the teacher; in addition, it tends to convey, whether intended or not, a more authoritarian, rigid teacher position.

As you examine your classroom, also consider its potential for delineating areas for different activities. Have you arranged desks, room dividers, and cabinets to provide the maximum flexibility in the use of the space? Are there areas in which two or three students can work together? Are there more quiet, private spaces to which a student can retreat, perhaps to read or just relax for a few moments? I remember a classroom in which staff and parents built the equivalent of a small loft that allowed students to take a break and also to feel a little more grown up as they gazed at adults from a higher vantage point.

Does your arrangement of classroom space complement and reinforce or work against effective teaching and learning? Are you able to provide a semicircular space for storytelling and reading and a circular space for certain classroom discussions? Is there a space conducive to your holding a relatively private conversation with one or two students?

I recognize that some of you are fortunate to be housed in classrooms that permit a flexible use of space. For those of you who are not, rather than becoming discouraged, attempt to focus on those limited areas of space that are within your control. You may be surprised to find that you and your students can probably do more in the arrangement of classroom space than might be obvious at first. It is important to remember that how you design your room is a reflection of your views about teaching and about the kinds of relationships you wish to nurture in the classroom.

Over the years, I have become increasingly convinced that we can turn the school's physical space into a vibrant psychological space in countless ways, a psychological space in which students feel comfortable and secure, in which they can learn more effectively, relate to others more satisfactorily, and see their accomplishments displayed everywhere. Motivation, self-worth, and enjoyment will thrive in such a psychological space.

Chapter Ten

TO OFFER ENCOURAGEMENT AND AVOID A "PRAISE DEFICIT"

"In the fifth grade, I had written a poem which my teacher had adored. She asked me to write it on a large piece of poster board and convinced me to send it to Reader's Digest.*"*

"In the first grade, the teacher would always begin the day with a positive comment for all students."

"My seventh-grade science teacher sent home a progress report to tell my parents how well I was doing."

When I first began offering workshops about self-esteem to parents and teachers, I emphasized the need to provide positive feedback to children and adolescents. Although this advice may sound basic to fostering self-esteem, I learned that many adults often failed to include this strategy in their relationship with others. I worked with many parents who expressed the belief that if their children did something right, it was expected and not much had to be said, but if their children did something wrong, punishment would follow. In questioning some of these parents, they either told me that they often just forgot about giving praise or they voiced concern that praise might result in their children becoming conceited.

I spoke with heads of businesses and discovered that for some a similar attitude about positive feedback existed. I recall one company president who told me, "My workers know what's expected of them and if they don't do what's expected, they'll hear from me." I asked if they heard from him when they did what was expected. He looked surprised and much to my astonishment questioned the need for positive feedback to motivate staff who were already getting paid.

In my contact with teachers and administrators, I also found that a lack of positive feedback was all too prevalent in schools. Teachers frequently said it would be easier to offer praise to students if they received such feedback themselves from parents and administrators. Administrators, in turn, shared with me the lack of appreciation they receive from parents, teachers, and school committee members.

Common sense suggests that people welcome realistic words of encouragement and appreciation more than they do words of criticism. Common sense also suggests that people will experience criticism as helpful and constructive when it comes from someone who has also taken the time in the past to offer positive feedback. Yet, the practices of too many individuals seem to run contrary to this logic.

To Overcome a "Praise Deficit"

Although I was readily aware of the importance of positive feedback and encouragement as a self-esteem strategy, this awareness was heightened when I read an article in which the author used the phrase "praise deficit" in describing the style shown by some parents towards their children.[1] While I prefer the concept of encouragement over praise, reading the words "praise deficit" for the first time triggered an important memory from when I was in training as a postdoctoral fellow in clinical psychology. At the beginning of my training year, I had been asked to speak at a clinical meeting. I was not yet accustomed to speaking in public and was rather apprehensive about doing so.

I spent hours in preparation as well as hours contemplating all of the possible questions that might be asked. Finally, the day arrived. I made my presentation and thought that it went relatively well, but I had to leave immediately for another meeting and thus did not have the opportunity to receive comments. When I returned to my office later in the afternoon, I found a note in my mailbox from one of my supervisors. While it probably took him no more than a few seconds to write, it was to have a significant impact on me, establishing a very positive tone for my entire postdoctoral training. The note simply read, "You did a great job today, Bob."

As I thought about this event from my postdoctoral experience, I wondered why its memory had been prompted by my reading the words "praise deficit." Certainly the description "praise deficit" could be applied to those many individuals mentioned earlier in this chapter who often fail to provide positive feedback to others. However, in thinking about the note from my supervisor and the impact it had on me, I realized that there are some forms of praise or encouragement, such as embodied in my supervisor's note, that are so powerful that they are forever remembered by the recipient of the praise—they truly become our indelible memories.

I wondered what it was about my supervisor's note that injected it with such force. My curiosity was more than academic since I thought that if I could better understand what made the note so powerful, I could use and harness its energy in other situations. I believe that what made the note so memorable was its total unexpectedness, so that when it arrived, I experienced it as a message of genuine caring and respect—my supervisor had gone out of his way for me. I thought about the importance of always finding opportunities to let children and adolescents know when we appreciate things they have said or done, to commend them for their efforts and accomplishments. In addition, I became convinced that we must find opportunities to convey well-deserved praise and encouragement at times when it is not anticipated or in forms that are somewhat unique. Often the unexpected or unusual expressions of appreciation are most remembered since they do not follow a predictable script, and thus they stand out.

To Feel Appreciated

Think for a moment about times when you were children or today as educators that you have felt most encouraged and appreciated. What made you feel that way? In an earlier chapter, I referred to an anonymous questionnaire that I ask teachers to complete. Its third question reads, "Please list a couple of things that enhance your effectiveness and self-esteem as an educator." I have been impressed by the number of teachers whose responses reflect the impact of unexpected feedback from others, such as another teacher complimenting them for a class project they designed, another teacher asking for advice, a brief note of thanks from a student or parent, a note of appreciation from a supervisor or principal.

I understand very well the power of such feedback whether captured in my supervisor's note or in a brief memo I received from one of the administrators of McLean Hospital, who after reviewing a brochure of an upcoming conference I had organized said that it looked like a very impressive program. I had not expected his memo, but after I received it I felt like framing it. In yet another example, a hospital administrator wrote some words of thanks at the bottom of a form letter announcing our annual salary increase. I was pleased to learn of a raise in salary, but was especially touched by his brief, personal comments. My reactions to these situations reminded me that regardless of what point we are at in our lives and professional careers, it is an uplifting experience to hear words of appreciation.

We all enjoy receiving expressions of thanks and encouragement, but unfortunately, we often neglect to find the few moments to express our appreciation to others. In my workshops, I ask teachers to reflect upon the ways in which they provide support and encouragement for each other. I believe that such support among educators helps create an atmosphere in school that more easily allows teachers to overcome a praise deficit in their relationship with their students. Think about a colleague or supervisor from whom you have learned and whose input you have found valuable. Imagine what would happen if you sent a note of thanks to that individual. Even a brief communication can serve as the catalyst for the emergence of a more supportive school environment in which everyone's self-esteem and motivation are reinforced.

There are many ways in which praise deficits can be overcome and an air of encouragement can permeate all of our endeavors. For example, following through on the other self-esteem strategies highlighted in this book will help students feel encouraged and appreciated. Respecting the individuality of students, creating an atmosphere of belonging, providing special times, promoting a sense of psychological space, offering opportunities for decision making and problem solving, helping students learn to deal with mistakes: all these strategies serve to communicate messages that counteract praise deficits.

The Power of Seemingly Small Gestures

A number of the positive memories I have gathered from teachers as they recall their own days as students include situations in which one of their teachers wrote a particularly encouraging comment on a test or paper. Often this action was experienced as genuine caring since it went beyond what was expected. I remember an English teacher I had in high school. We were given an assignment of selecting and interpreting several poems. Poetry was not my forte, and I felt some apprehension about doing an acceptable job. I spent many hours reading different poems, selecting those that had some appeal for me, and then struggling to understand and write about the possible meanings housed in these poems.

On the day the papers were to be returned, my teacher

caught me for a few minutes before class and told me that
she was very impressed by my analysis of the poems,
thoughts that were reflected in the many comments that she
wrote on my paper. Even some of her comments that I would
have previously experienced as negative I now saw as
constructive. I will always remember her finding a few
minutes to talk with me and how this seemingly small
gesture increased my confidence and motivation. This kind
of small gesture of encouragement can become part of our
modus operandi without the expenditure of much time or
effort. A few extra words on a student's test or paper may
take us several seconds to write, but the impact on the
student and our classroom climate will be long-lasting.

Another powerful memory for me goes back to the sixth
grade. Each student in the class was assigned a product to
research, and I chose the coffee bean. (I'm not certain why.)
Our sixth-grade teacher always encouraged taking risks and
being creative. Thus, I decided that rather than write what
could turn out to be a rather dull paper about coffee
beans—where they came from and how they were
processed—I would borrow from the format of one of the
most popular television series of that time, "Dragnet." I
wrote my paper as a detective story in which Sgt. Joe Friday
is called upon to solve the murder of a man whose coffee has
been poisoned; the plot involved Friday tracing the coffee
bean back to its origin, thereby providing me with a format
for describing the life of the bean.

I received very positive comments about my paper, and
our teacher arranged for several of us to read our stories at a
school assembly. What a pleasant surprise when I was
introduced, and my teacher played the theme music from
the "Dragnet" show! He had taken the time to tape the
music to enhance my presentation.

I once visited an elementary school whose lobby was filled
with the photos of children attached to posters designating a
variety of weekly awards. The awards included recognition in
many areas such as academic success, academic
improvement, and school service; in some instances, a class

picture was included to signify class accomplishments. The students were very proud of these posters, and in my discussion with the principal, he informed me that the school attempted to ensure that at some point during the school year every student's photo (either individually or in a group) appeared on a poster. In this regard, Michael Rutter's study of British schools found that student performance and behavior were better in those schools that emphasized "public commendation for work and behavior, as by praising individual children in school assemblies or other meetings."[2]

The Teacher's Relationship With Parents

Another form of overcoming a praise deficit concerns a teacher's relationship with parents. Many parents with whom I have spoken feel that when they receive unexpected feedback from teachers, it often involves something negative that their child has done. I know the impact on parents when a teacher calls or writes to provide positive comments. (In my presentations to parent groups, I often encourage parents to communicate similar appreciation to teachers.) I recall one parent who was frequently called by the school about her fourth-grade son's behavioral problems, problems that had become so pronounced on the school bus that the mother had to pick her son up each afternoon and drive him home. She recalls waiting for him one afternoon. She saw him running out of the building and then spotted the teacher running a short distance behind him. The mother told me she was convinced that the teacher was either trying to stop her son or running out to report something negative. "As I saw the teacher approaching, I had the urge to put my foot on the accelerator and drive off, since I didn't want to hear any more bad news," she said.

Reason prevailed, and she did not flee the scene. Upon reaching the car, the teacher said that she wanted to let the mother know how well the last couple of days had gone and the improvement her son was starting to show. As the mother told me what had transpired, it was evident that she greatly appreciated that her son's teacher had run out to give her this feedback. She and the teacher formed a strong bond; the teacher's alliance with the boy was also reinforced.

To Counteract Knee-Jerk Reactions

One point deserves special mention in terms of the importance of expressing praise, encouragement, and appreciation in an unexpected form. (Of course, such feedback should also be a regular feature of the classroom routine.) As teachers have so often observed, many students with low self-esteem appear to immediately reject positive feedback. The script for these students seems to include a knee-jerk reaction that pushes us away when we praise them. It might seem puzzling at first glance that students who feel so inadequate should reject genuine positive comments. They appear to dismiss ideas that do not fit into their self-image, as negative as this self-image might be.

When we give feedback to these children, our efforts will be successful only if we help short-circuit these automatic negative reactions. That is why I might send brief notes to certain patients, complimenting them on productive efforts they have made and achievements they have realized. I find that notes, compared with spoken words, are less likely to be immediately rejected. Another technique I sometimes use—as long as I believe it will come across in a caring way—is to say to patients that I have something to tell them, but I'm not certain I should. When they ask what it is, I reply (with a twinkle in my eye) that I am hesitant to tell them since I think they will say I'm wrong and not believe me. Eventually with the prodding of the patients, I offer my positive feedback, and I often hear them say, "You're right, I don't believe you." However, a tinge of playfulness is typically in their voice in reaction to my own playfulness, and they seem more willing to consider my positive comments.

Self-respect and learning will thrive in school environments in which both students and staff receive well-deserved encouragement and praise. Regardless of our age or our professional status or how good we feel about ourselves, it is always nice to be appreciated and recognized.

Self-esteem teachers realize that by taking the initiative, by finding ways to provide such positive feedback to their students and colleagues and administrators, they can develop a school climate in which praise deficits disappear and in which everyone serves as a source of encouragement for others.

In closing, I wish to mention that some teachers have told me of the fun they have experienced when leaving positive notes for colleagues and students or offering commendations in public. They often describe what they do as contagious, so that others soon follow their lead, offering their own expressions of appreciation and encouragement. An atmosphere of warmth, fun, and playfulness is likely to result, providing the nourishment for increased motivation, learning, and self-esteem.

Chapter Eleven

TO DEVELOP RESPONSIBILITY AND MAKE A CONTRIBUTION

"In the sixth grade, my teacher helped me to feel I had made a significant contribution to a class newspaper with my postage-stamp-size poem."

"In the fourth grade, I was given the opportunity to 'teach' an art lesson to a group of several younger students."

In my self-esteem workshops for educators I pose the following question: "If I were to ask your students what they feel they contribute to the well-being of their school, what would their answers be?" Reflect for a moment how you think your students would answer this question. Responses I have received from teachers vary greatly from silence, to comments that they have never really thought about this question before, to statements that students are in school to learn specific academic content and not to contribute to the well-being of the school, to general remarks such as "Our students are responsible for showing respect in school," to more specific examples such as "Our students assist in the office" or "They tutor younger children in math and reading."

I ask this question for two related reasons. First, I believe that a basic ingredient of self-esteem is a feeling of responsibility for what occurs in our lives. Consequently, as educators we should strive to provide for our students opportunities to assume responsibilities in the school setting. Second, based on research findings, discussions I have had with students, and the responses to the first item on my anonymous questionnaire for teachers ("Please describe briefly an experience that you had with an educator when you were a student that reinforced your self-esteem."), I believe that responsibilities expressed in the form of making a contribution are especially potent in fostering self-esteem.[1] I would assert further that overall behavior, motivation, and academic achievement will be enhanced in those schools that engage students in what can be called "contributory activities." In this regard, I am reminded of psychologist Urie Bronfenbrenner's recommendation that schools implement a "curriculum for caring," offering students the chance to learn about and engage in acts of caring with such populations as "old people, younger children, the sick and the lonely."[2]

Memories and Research About
Responsibilities and Contributions

Think of your own experiences as a student and the ways in which you felt you contributed to the school. I recall that as a sixth grader, I was appointed a street crossing guard and proudly wore my badge as I assisted younger children to arrive safely at the school building. And who could forget Mrs. Roth in junior high school asking me to draw signs and posters? Still later, I served as a tutor during my junior and senior years of high school. I can remember the pride and accomplishment I felt performing all of these activities— feelings that increased my enjoyment of school and my motivation to learn.

The nature of my positive images of school is not unique. I was impressed with how many of the positive memories described by teachers on my questionnaire involved responsibilities that helped them gain a strong sense that they had made a contribution. The first two chapters of this book hold several examples of these memories such as: "In the third grade, I was chosen to help get the milk and straws."

We all know how satisfying it can be to feel that we are truly making a difference, that we are contributing. The importance of reinforcing this feeling in school is supported by Michael Rutter's research in England. Rutter found:

> Ample opportunities for children to take responsibility and to participate in the running of their school lives appear conducive to good attainments, attendance, and behavior. Thus, academic outcome was better in schools where a high proportion of pupils had been form captain, homework monitor, or some equivalent position. The same applied to a high proportion of pupils who had taken a special part of some responsibility in school assemblies, house, or year meetings. . . . It was striking that the schools in which children were expected to take care of their own things had better outcomes with respect to attendance, behavior, and delinquency. . . . There is some indication that holding positions of responsibility at school may help students' commitment to education.[3]

Responsibilities and Contributions in School

I have worked with students who were turned off to school, who felt that school was the place where their deficits rather than their strengths were spotlighted. One of my interventions to offset this negative outlook has been to collaborate with teachers in developing responsibilities and contributory activities for students that nurture the feeling "I have something worthwhile to offer this school." These responsibilities can be created on an individual or group basis, keeping in mind the interests and developmental level of the students.

One seventh-grade teacher told me that his learning environment improved when he developed twenty-five responsibilities in his class and informed the students at the beginning of the school year that this was their class and he needed their assistance in fulfilling these responsibilities. In describing this intervention to me, the teacher said he could immediately sense a difference in the atmosphere of each of his classes. Students appeared increasingly responsible and motivated and, in turn, he felt more excited and satisfied about the impact he was having.

In another example of this self-esteem strategy, Albina Gaudino and Michele Tamaren discussed how visually handicapped adolescents who were slow learners produced piggy banks to sell and sponsored a bake sale and a raffle, with the proceeds going to a needy family; it was noted that these activities enchanced the students' self-esteem and reinforced the many academic skills that were involved in the project.[4] Mary Sarver reported the emotional and cognitive benefits of having students between the ages of eight and twelve plan and take care of a school garden in which flowers and vegetables were grown, observing, "It was not at all surprising that many of my students asked to take some of their harvest from the garden to their other teachers. The flowers and vegetables they had grown were silent proof they could succeed."[5]

I visited an elementary school and talked with some special education students. Before I left, they proudly gave me a colorful button that had the inscription "SOS, Serving Our School" printed on it. A special education teacher in the school had become intrigued by the notion of contributory activities and developed this SOS program in which each student was scheduled at some point during the week to be available to perform various errands for the school staff (for instance, delivering a memo). The importance accorded this program was very evident when I entered the resource room and was greeted by a large, carefully designed SOS schedule on the wall that indicated when each student was on duty. In my discussion with students involved in the SOS program, it was evident that the program was a source of pride and achievement for them and that they looked forward to the contributions they could make as SOS participants.

Another contributory activity involves the use of students as tutors, a widely used practice that has been found to benefit both the student who is doing the tutoring as well as the student receiving instruction.[6] I am familiar with schools that have entire classes spend some time each week working with younger children. In this regard, I am reminded of the impressive results of the Valued Youth Partnership Program[7] developed in San Antonio in which the dropout rate of young adolescents was cut significantly, primarily by involving them as tutors for younger children. The report issued by the Carnegie Council on Adolescent Development, *Turning Points: Preparing American Youth for the 21st Century*, commended this program, noting:

> A rise in tutors' self-esteem is the most noticeable effect of the program. . . . As a result, only 2 percent of all tutors have dropped out of school. This is remarkable, given that all of these students had been held back twice or more and were reading at least two grade levels below their current grade placement. Disciplinary problems have become less severe, grades have improved, and attendance of tutors has soared.[8]

In my clinical practice, I often recommend the use of tutoring as a strategy to motivate students. In an earlier chapter, I described a sixth-grade girl whose failure to do her own homework and meet class requirements was remedied to a large extent by engaging her as a tutor for first and second graders—another example of the beneficial power of making a contribution. The strategy of delegating responsibility was also used for a kindergarten child who typically would not listen to the teacher when requested to come in from the playground after recess. This child was asked to become the "recess monitor," a position that required him to return to the classroom a little before his classmates and hold the door for them. This was presented as an important task, and he handled it very well without having to be reminded to come in. Obviously, when we ask students to become tutors or to assume other responsibilities, we must also provide them with whatever

training and supervision are needed to maximize their
success.

To Become a Pet Monitor

I will always remember Billy, a nine-year-old boy with
learning problems and low self-esteem, whose main ways of
coping were to strike out angrily at other children or to hide
behind the bushes outside the school building. At one point
during our first session, I asked Billy why he hid behind the
bushes. He responded rather directly, informing me that he
"liked the bushes better than school." At this point I could
have entered into a discussion of the relative merits of
bushes versus schools. Instead, I decided to learn what he
perceived to be his islands of competence. I asked what he
enjoyed doing and thought that he did relatively well. He
responded that he enjoyed taking care of his pet dog. With
his permission, I mentioned Billy's fondness for animals to
the school principal. I asked the principal if the school might
not benefit from the presence of a "pet monitor," offering a
quickly conceived job description.

The following day the principal saw Billy and asked if he
might be interested in becoming the school's first pet
monitor, even handing Billy the equivalent of a pet monitor
"union card" that he had created. When Billy wondered what
a pet monitor did, the principal said that to begin with, Billy
would be expected to come to school ten minutes early each
day to take care of a rabbit the school had recently
purchased; the principal added that he thought Billy could
do a good job and that his assuming the position would be
very helpful.

Billy accepted the offer and handled his duties in a very
responsible way, in marked contrast to his history with
academic requirements. Within a short time, he began to
take care of other pets in addition to the rabbit. Billy's
teacher expressed how impressed she was with his
knowledge of pets and engaged him in writing a manual
about animal care. Billy had always been reluctant to write,
but in this instance his hesistancy disappeared since he felt

more confident and recognized that he had information to offer. The manual was bound and became part of the school library. In addition, by the end of the school year Billy "lectured" in every classroom in the building about taking care of pets.

Very importantly, Billy's aggressive outbursts and his avoidance of the school building decreased significantly after he assumed the pet monitor position. Various factors contributed to his increasing confidence, but perhaps the most important was being offered a responsibility that resonated with his interests and provided him with an opportunity to display an island of competence. Billy's teacher and principal had been willing to take a risk and change the script, and the results were very encouraging. It was also very beneficial to have the teacher and principal work closely together, but even if this kind of collaboration is not possible, teachers can still be effective in providing contributory activities for students.

It is not unusual for some educators to ask what happens if other children want to become pet monitors or attendance monitors or tutors. My answer is that each student in a classroom—whether demonstrating problems or not—deserves the opportunity to engage in activities that convey a feeling of contributing. Such activities can become an integral part of the curriculum and interwoven with the teaching of academic skills.

The Benefits of Cooperative Learning

Before ending this chapter, I wish to call attention to a form of learning and instruction that in many ways is rooted in the self-esteem strategy of providing responsibilities and making a contribution: cooperative learning.[9]

Assuming responsibilities and contributing to a group goal are essential parts of cooperative learning. Competition among students and the use of tracking or placing students in homogeneous ability groups are minimized when cooperative learning is used. This is important to remember since a number of research findings suggest that tracking does not help high achievers and has the potential for hurting average and slow learners. For example, a Massachusetts Board of Education report, titled *Structuring Schools for Student Success: A Focus on Ability Grouping*, noted that "there is little evidence that ability grouping or tracking improves academic achievement, while overwhelming evidence exists that ability grouping retards the academic progress of students in low- and middle-ability groupings."[10] The report advocated the use of cooperative group learning since such an approach ". . .views heterogeneity as a resource rather than a problem, and has been found to increase achievement for all students, while diminishing the achievement gap among White, Black, and Hispanic students. It has also resulted in cross-racial friendships and in better attitudes of students towards different racial groups."[11]

The Carnegie report, *Turning Points: Preparing American Youth for the 21st Century*, also criticized the practice of tracking while praising cooperative learning and cross-age tutoring, two approaches that utilize the self-esteem strategy of providing responsibilities and helping make a contribution. As the Carnegie report observes:

> In cooperative learning situations, all students contribute to the group effort because students receive group rewards as well as individual grades. High achievers deepen their understanding of material by explaining it to lower achievers; those of lower achievement receive immediate tutoring from their peers and gain a sense of accomplishment by suggesting solutions to problems. . . . Cooperative learning has been shown to help students to learn course material more rapidly than working alone.[12]

Robert Slavin, one of the foremost researchers on the topic of cooperative learning, has written that this form of learning increases students' self-esteem, promotes interest in school and student attendance, and increases the ability to work effectively with others.[13] Given the positive findings that have been found when cooperative learning is introduced in the classroom, it would appear to be an educational practice that deserves increased attention and use by teachers.

As is evident, teachers can implement in many different ways the strategy of delegating responsibilities, especially responsibilities that help students feel that they are making a contribution to their school. Any of us would lose our enthusiasm and motivation if placed in an environment in which we felt our presence made little difference. The self-esteem teacher is very aware of the importance of engaging students in meaningful classroom and school responsibilities that foster a sense of belonging and group alliance and that constantly remind students that they are having a positive impact in school.

Chapter Twelve

TO LEARN FROM
MISTAKES AND FAILURES

"After failing chemistry as a junior in high school, I took it over as a senior. My second chemistry teacher was extremely patient and encouraging. I received B's and A's the second time around."

"I remember a teacher who encouraged me and worked with me after I repeated a grade."

I believe that the fear of making mistakes and feeling embarrassed and humiliated is one of the most formidable barriers to taking risks, to meeting challenges, to learning. The ways in which we deal with mistakes and failures are intimately linked to our self-esteem. Students with a positive self-image are more likely to perceive mistakes as experiences from which to learn rather than feel defeated by, while those with a negative self-image are often so distressed by failure that they flee from the situation, relying on counterproductive coping maneuvers.

To understand more clearly how our students feel, it's helpful to look at our own reactions when placed in a situation where we might make a mistake. For example, many of us, when attending conferences or inservice workshops, do not find it easy either to respond to questions raised by the presenter or to ask questions of our own. Even if we possess relatively high self-esteem, we are not totally free from nagging doubts about making a mistake or revealing what we don't know in front of other people. I was not surprised to learn about a study that found that the fear of speaking in public was rated as the number one fear experienced by people—we become very anxious when we feel that our vulnerabilities or weaknesses are exposed.

We would all love to teach in a classroom in which fears and doubts were minimized, in which students would be less hesitant to attempt new and difficult tasks, would be more secure in offering opinions and answers and more open to engaging in discussions without worries of being judged or ridiculed. What a learning environment that would be! The self-esteem teacher can create such an environment.

To Learn From Strikeouts

At all of my self-esteem workshops, I read a quote about dealing with mistakes. It was written by a baseball player named Willie Stargell, a man who was elected into the Baseball Hall of Fame for his performance as a Pittsburgh Pirate. In an article that appeared in *Parade Magazine* in 1983, Stargell described what he had learned from playing baseball. His words go far beyond the baseball field and reflect a philosophy of life toward which we could all strive. He wrote:

> Baseball also taught me what I need to survive in the world. . . . The game has given me the patience to learn and succeed. As much as I was known for my homers, I also was known for my strikeouts. The strikeout is the ultimate failure, and I struck out 1936 times. . . . But I'm proud of my strikeouts, for I feel that to succeed, one must first fail; and the more you fail, the more you learn about succeeding. The person who has never tried and failed will never succeed. Each time I walked away from the plate after a strikeout, I learned something. Whether it was about my swing, not seeing the

ball, the pitcher or the weather conditions, I learned something. My success is the product of the knowledge extracted from my failures. The key to surviving a failure is to bend, not break. At times, I bent like a palm tree in a hurricane, but I never broke.[1]

I remember that the first time I read Stargell's words I experienced a little guilt, realizing that I didn't always feel like a palm tree in a hurricane after making a mistake, but more like a tree that had fallen. I also recognized that what Stargell expressed could be understood as a goal for which to strive similar to the following sentiments found in the California report *Toward a State of Esteem*:

> Mistakes are a natural part of life. We learn by experimenting; mistakes and failures can be important parts of our learning process. Einstein flunked grade school mathematics. Edison tried over 9,000 kinds of filament before he found one that would work in a light bulb. Walt Disney went bankrupt five times before he built Disneyland. If we accept our setbacks, we can continue to risk, learn, and move on with excitement and satisfaction.[2]

To Acknowledge Fears of Failing

What can we do from the first day of class to reinforce the feelings expressed by Stargell and the California Self-Esteem Task Force? How do we convey the message to our students that mistakes are not only accepted, but totally expected? I believe that since fears of failing and being humiliated are present to a greater or lesser extent in most students and will play a role in their performance in school, then these fears should be openly discussed at the beginning of the school year rather than remaining powerful and influential, but unacknowledged.

It is not easy to initiate a discussion in public about the fears we have pertaining to making mistakes and feeling humiliated. Since we cannot expect our students to raise this topic, the task falls on our shoulders. For instance, what might happen if at some point during the first or second day of school you asked your students, "Who feels that they will probably make a mistake in class this year?" and before anyone can respond you raise your own hand? You could then ask students why they thought you brought up the issue of making mistakes, and use their answers as a launching pad to discuss how fears of making mistakes and feeling humiliated in front of other students interfere with offering opinions and answers, engaging in class discussions, and learning.

You might also ask students if they could recall a situation in the past in which they had made a mistake either in school or elsewhere and how other people reacted. You might share an experience you had from your childhood that involved failing. You could then ask the students how they might respond to each other's mistakes in this class. "Should we laugh and make fun of the person? How would that make the person feel? Should we say to the person it's okay to make mistakes? If you make a mistake, what would you like other students to do? How would you like me to respond to mistakes you make in class or on a test?" You might continue the discussion by asking students what they should do if they don't understand something that is being taught. "Should you raise your hand and ask questions? Have you ever felt funny about asking questions? Do you worry that it shows that you are having trouble learning something that you believe other students have learned more easily?"

Some people might wonder if this kind of discussion belongs in a classroom and if it will accomplish anything. I believe that the fear of making mistakes and being embarrassed is so potent, and yet typically unacknowledged, that unless it is made public it will interfere with the creation of a nonthreatening classroom environment in which learning and self-esteem can thrive.

Obviously, the discussion I have just recommended is but one way to minimize the negative impact of not grasping immediately the information being taught or of making mistakes. I heard about one teacher who on the first day of class placed a small, empty jar on her desk and handed her students small rocks. She told them that whenever a student "caught" her making a mistake, the student was to place one of the rocks in the jar; when the jar was filled she would provide the class with a treat. What a powerful message this teacher communicated about feeling comfortable with making mistakes!

To Help Students Take Risks

I believe that a primary task teachers face at the start of the school year is to establish a level of comfort for students that will permit them to take risks as they learn. The negative memories recalled by teachers on my questionnaire frequently concerned feeling demeaned and belittled either for giving incorrect answers or for not understanding the material being taught: "I was told by a grade-school teacher that my answer was stupid." "My algebra teacher accused me of asking questions to disrupt the class when in truth I was seeking understanding." "In the sixth grade, my teacher informed me that because I was in the gifted program, I would not be allowed to make any spelling mistakes." "In elementary school I asked a question and the teacher said, 'Weren't you listening? I just answered that!' I rarely asked questions after that." How we respond to the mistakes of our students as well as to our own mistakes is an important determinant of the classroom climate we establish.

I will always recall my fifth-grade teacher for how demeaning she was and how little I learned in her class. About the third week of school, she wrote a list of spelling words on the board. I noticed that she misspelled a word and thought that she had done this on purpose to see who might notice the error. I raised my hand and politely said that I thought one of the words was spelled incorrectly. I actually had expected her to compliment me by saying, "There's a bright boy. He saw that this word was not spelled correctly." Instead, she appeared angry as she corrected the error on the board. A little later as I was going out to recess she called me over and angrily told me that I should never correct her in front of the other children again, that it was disrespectful. I must admit I felt like crying, I felt like hitting her, I felt

like running from her class never to return. I disliked her
class for the rest of the year, an attitude that certainly
interfered with what I was able to learn.

My sixth-grade year was much different. Our teacher was
very encouraging and helped me feel that mistakes were a
natural part of learning and succeeding. He did this in so
many ways. I remember an abstract art project the class was
doing. Although I enjoyed art, my final product was not very
good. My teacher could see I was disappointed. He placed his
hand on my shoulder and said that it was fine to begin again
if I wished to do so. My second attempt produced more
satisfying results. I also recall an occasion when our class was
playing another class in punch ball. (This was a popular game
in Brooklyn in which, instead of hitting a ball with a bat, the
hitter threw a rubber ball up in the air and hit it with a
clenched fist.) The first two times I was up, I had hit the ball
with little force. My teacher was very encouraging and
basically told me not to worry. The third time up I hit the
ball over an outfielder's head for a home run. Perhaps I
would have done this even without my teacher's words of
support, but his input was very reassuring. I am certain that
if my third attempt at hitting the ball had proven as
unsuccessful as the first two, he would have been there to
tell me not to get discouraged. During my sixth-grade year, I
learned a great deal from my teacher about bouncing back
from unsuccessful efforts.

Your Style of Correcting Students' Work

Take a moment to reflect upon your interactions with
students and the extent to which you communicate the
message that is being advocated in this chapter: that
mistakes are an integral part of the learning process. Focus
on the manner in which you give feedback to students about
their work. For instance, when you grade a paper do you
indicate points subtracted for incorrect answers or points
earned for correct answers? One teacher told me that she
typically took points off in red ink until she placed herself in
the shoes of her students and realized how negatively they

might experience that practice. Points taken off often highlight weaknesses at the expense of strengths and thus may be more likely to reinforce a feeling of failure.

I am not suggesting that we avoid calling errors to the attention of our students; not to acknowledge errors would be counterproductive since it would fail to provide students with important feedback about their performance, feedback that would indicate areas that required further reinforcement. Instead, I am saying that we should ensure that we highlight what students know and then focus on helping them develop more effective learning techniques to increase their skills and knowledge in areas in which they are not as efficient. This approach should not be interpreted as a mind game we play with students that simply involves adding rather than subtracting points. Rather, it is a strategy predicated on minimizing the negative impact of making mistakes and enhancing the process of learning. As Anne Meyer has so aptly emphasized:

> Teachers who respond to errors by immediately offering the correct solution or calling on another student convey the message that errors are failures and that they are interested in performance outcomes (i.e., teaching children the right answer) rather than process (i.e., teaching children how to approach problems). Conversely, teachers who respond to errors by allowing children time to try again, offering clues, and suggesting alternative strategies convey the message that errors are a constructive part of the learning process and evoke no negative judgments about ability. . . . Teachers who regard themselves as guides and aids rather than judges are likely to convey this attitude to children, promoting students' ability to turn to them and seek assistance without feelings of shame.[3]

As you lessen the fears and shame associated with making mistakes and failing, you will provide students with an environment that truly encourages taking risks and meeting challenges. Such an environment will be permeated with excitement, satisfaction, classroom magic—and learning.

Chapter Thirteen

TO PROVIDE CHOICES
AND REINFORCE
A SENSE OF OWNERSHIP

*"As a first grader, I used to leave school because
I had nothing to do when I finished my work.
After a conference, I was allowed to choose
something else to do when I finished rather than
just wait for everyone to catch up."*

*"My sixth-grade teacher always gave us choices
about books to read and where to hang reports
in the room. He respected our opinions."*

I have already mentioned several questions I ask educators
who attend my self-esteem workshops. Another is: "If I were
to ask your students what choices they feel they are given in
your classroom, how would they answer?" Think about what
your students might say if asked this question. What choices
have been built into your classroom routine?

It may seem obvious why I would focus on the question of
choices in a workshop about self-esteem. I believe that all of
us benefit from having some choice or autonomy in what we
do. To be given a meaningful choice promotes a sense of

ownership and personal control, which in turn reinforces self-esteem and motivation. Margaret Cohen, discussing strategies for increasing motivation in the classroom, noted, "The most critical elements in motivation enhancement are ownership and choice. Ownership guarantees investment in an activity, and offering choices serves to facilitate this investment."[1]

Although the feeling that we have some choice in what occurs in our lives is very important in building motivation and self-esteem, many teachers have honestly shared with me that they have never systematically built in choices for students to make in their classrooms; yet, they also acknowledge that their own motivation is increased when they feel they are provided with options. Unfortunately, many students I have interviewed do not feel they have any choice or ownership in school—instead they experience school as something they must do, something that is imposed upon them. This feeling lessens a student's motivation to learn.

Choices and the Classroom Routine

I always advocate that as part of their regular classroom routine, teachers build in choices for students to make. I remember an American history teacher I had in high school. On the first day of class he informed us, "I plan to prepare you for life." I thought, "How exciting, being prepared for life!"—although I wasn't certain what he meant. Then he distributed his homework assignments, which were so comprehensive that I said to myself, "Now I know what he means—it will take a lifetime to complete this work."

I learned a great deal from this rather demanding and stimulating teacher. One thing I recall about his class was the choices he gave us: "Your test is in two weeks. Let's vote on who would like to have it on Friday and who would like to take it on the following Monday. It's your choice." "Your paper is due at the end of the month. Let's vote on who would like the extra weekend to turn it in. It's your choice." Never once did he give us the option of taking or not taking the test or doing or not doing the paper. Nor did he present individual options for each student, which could have been unmanageable for him. Yet, by offering a choice between two dates for a test being taken or a paper being turned in, I believe that we all felt more of a sense of ownership.

Reinforcing Self-Determination and
Minimizing Power Struggles

With the existence of choices, students feel more in control and are less likely to resist doing different tasks in school. Choices promote a feeling of self-determination and typically will minimize power struggles. One of my favorite examples of this occurred with a six-year-old boy whom I was seeing in therapy. He was both learning disabled and a perfectionist. Since his learning disabilities prevented him from writing his letters and numbers in the perfect style that he desired, he decided not to write. While other children were writing, he coped with the threat of failure by getting out of his seat and fooling around, much to the dismay of his teacher.

Attempts at both reward and punishment were ineffective. By the time I became involved, it seemed obvious that a power struggle existed between the teacher and my patient. The teacher and I discussed the negative script that was operating. We talked about ways of altering this script and modifying my patient's self-defeating ways of coping. After some deliberation, we developed a plan that we hoped would lessen the power struggle and enhance my patient's feeling of ownership for his education. The teacher spoke with my patient and told him that she could see that he really did not like to write—an understatement, but at least it was empathic. She told him that perhaps one way she could help would be to let him select one "vacation day" each week when he did not have to write during writing time. She added that he would have to do something else, but not writing. She had a list of several alternative activities that he could engage in during his vacation day, all of which involved productive tasks.

A couple of days later I saw him in our regularly scheduled therapy session. He told me that the teacher was giving him a vacation day once a week from writing and that he could choose the day. I hesitantly asked him what he planned to do on the other four days. He said, "I'll write. I'm getting a vacation day." His complying with this intervention seemed to show that he really wanted to avoid a power struggle and that he wanted to attempt to write; the use of a choice permitted him to feel in control of the situation. By the beginning of the next school year, a vacation day was no longer necessary to have him complete his assignments.

This kind of intervention will not always work, but my experience has been that it is successful more often than we realize. When I describe an intervention such as this, it is not unusual for people to question whether I am giving in to a child and reinforcing negative behavior. As I mentioned in an earlier chapter, I do not view the intervention as capitulating to a child's unrealistic demands, but rather as modifying a negative script. When I am asked what would happen if other students in the class requested a vacation day from writing, I respond by wondering what would happen if each student were given this option. Many might not take it, but perhaps those who did might work more productively on the other four days. Some educators may remain skeptical of providing this kind of choice to students, but I believe that for some children this approach would represent a change of script that would help motivate them in school.

In addition, the alternative activities or choices provided could always be those that fostered cognitive and emotional growth. These alternatives might even involve skills similar to the ones that are used in the regular activities, but in a form more acceptable and motivating to the child. For example, I had a teacher in elementary school who permitted us some choice in learning about fractions and percentages by saying we could do problems from the textbook or figure out the batting averages of our favorite players on the Brooklyn Dodgers. Interestingly, soon the alternative activity of figuring batting averages became the more prominent way in which we learned the math computations in question.

A Choice of Two Seats

A junior high school teacher once shared with me and other educators at a conference an amusing illustration involving choice. He was confronted one year with a rather active young adolescent who often moved around the room. Many attempts to tell this boy to remain seated failed. The teacher was becoming increasingly frustrated. One day he informed this student that from now on the student had a choice in his room. I thought that he was going to say that he told the boy, "Your choice is to remain seated or be expelled from the class." I was wrong. The teacher said to his student, "From now on you have a choice of two seats to sit in, one on that side of the room and the other on this side. (He pointed to the last seat on each of the aisles.) It's up to you where you want to sit, and you can move from one seat to the other."

I was puzzled by this strategy and asked, "Did it really help to offer two seats?"

The teacher responded, "Bob, psychologically it was one of the most important things I could do."

"It was?" I asked.

"Yes, because psychologically I told myself that whatever direction he was running toward, at least he was running toward his seat." All of us who heard this story laughed, prompted in part by this teacher's delightful delivery.

However, after learning that this strategy indeed helped the student, I reflected on how clever it was. Rather than continuing to tell a very active student to remain still, he found a way to permit this student to move around in a more controlled, focused manner. Also, the placement of the two seats at the back of the classroom minimized any disruption to the class when the student did switch seats, a behavior that lessened with time. Very importantly, the inclusion of a choice was an important determinant of this strategy's success.

So Many Choices to Offer

There are many other examples I could offer that illustrate the power of providing a choice and thereby communicating to students a feeling of control—examples that can more easily be incorporated into the classroom routine than perhaps the seemingly more extreme options of vacation days from writing or which of two chairs to occupy. Which book to read for a report, where in the classroom the reports can be displayed, and, within reason, the time during the day when certain skills are taught or projects are completed—these are but a few examples of providing choice.

In addition, I wonder if students would do their homework more readily and study more diligently in some subjects if they were given a choice of which of two assignments to do (for example, two similar lists of math problems, or a choice of which of two spelling lists to study this week and which to study the following week) or if they had the option of selecting eight out of ten math problems to do. In line with the strategy of delegating responsibilities and making a contribution, students could be given choices of the jobs they might assume in the classroom for a month. Or in concert with the strategy of psychological space, students might have a choice of where to paint a mural. The possibilities are endless.

Since some students may not experience or label the options you have provided as a choice, I believe it is important on occasion to actually use the word "choice" when offering these options. The use of the label may be especially helpful with younger children as a way of defining more precisely what is occurring. However, I should add that when my high school American history teacher used the word "choice," we did not feel as if he were treating us like little children, and I believe it helped reinforce a sense of control for us.

I have also witnessed the benefits of providing choices to children and adolescents in my therapy sessions. One patient

did not want to talk with me, but accepted the offer of a
five-minute "period of silence," during which he did not have
to say anything; he actually asked for two of these periods
but spoke with me the remainder of the session. After a
couple of months, offering these periods was no longer
necessary. Another child, who often attempted to leave our
sessions early, was given the choice of staying for the entire
time or leaving one or two minutes early. At first, he selected
the two-minute time—which was not only an improvement
on his earlier attempts to leave with fifteen or twenty
minutes remaining, but also lessened our struggles.

I continue to be impressed by examples in which
seemingly simple choices help create an environment in
which students feel in control of their learning. The
classroom of the self-esteem teacher is filled with different
choices that constantly say to students that their need for
self-determination is being respected and that they truly
possess some ownership for their classroom experiences.

Chapter Fourteen

TO PROVIDE OPPORTUNITIES FOR PROBLEM SOLVING AND DECISION MAKING

"I was in the ninth grade. The teacher trusted us to learn. He assigned interesting and challenging topics and let us work in small groups. He had a way of making everyone feel important. Part of it was his enthusiasm in class."

"My high school sociology teacher encouraged us to express our opinions even when quite different from hers. She verbalized her respect for us and her trust in us. On test days, she handed out the test and left the room."

The self-esteem strategy of providing opportunities for problem solving and decision making is very closely linked to the strategy described in the previous chapter concerning choices. In many ways, problem solving and decision making are interrelated processes that have their roots in making choices, but they typically require more complex thinking. Involved in the task of solving problems and making decisions are the abilities to articulate what the problem is, consider various options to solve the problem and the possible consequences of each option, select the option that appears most promising, try this option, and then learn from its outcome.

These are all necessary skills in developing a sense of autonomy and self-determination and thus are intimately related to a student's self-esteem and successful coping.

I believe that schools can provide a rich, fertile ground for nurturing problem-solving and decision-making skills. Once again, please reflect on your own classrooms. In what ways are you assisting and teaching students to solve problems? Are you permitting them to struggle at times with particular academic and social issues and problems and not immediately telling them what to do? How are you responding to their mistakes or to decisions with which you do not agree? What kinds of decisions are students permitted to make in school—and are they using thoughtful problem-solving skills to reach their decisions? We should remember that when students engage in the process of making decisions that affect their education and their school environment, they will nearly always feel an increasing sense of ownership and responsibility for what transpires. Also, as students acquire the skills to solve problems, they will be better equipped to manage the many challenges that will confront them, thereby enhancing their self-esteem and confidence.

Teachers and the Decision-Making Process

In the past few years, more and more attention has been directed to the question of who should be involved in making decisions in the school setting. Years ago it was not unusual for teachers to tell me that it was difficult to provide opportunities for students to make decisions when the teachers felt deprived of such opportunities themselves. However, that was before words and phrases such as "restructuring schools," "school-based management," and "teacher empowerment" became prominent parts of our lexicon, representing challenges to educational practices in which teachers had little control over what occurred in their own classrooms.

I have done several workshops sponsored by the Massachusetts Teachers Association, and in preparation for one of them, I was sent information about Carnegie School Programs. These programs have as a major goal encouraging "public schools to plan and develop innovative organizational and management systems at the school building level in order to improve students' learning and empower public school professionals." To achieve this goal Carnegie recommended that schools be restructured and that teachers be empowered with "a significant role in school decision-making" and "control over their work environment and work conditions." It was also recommended that parents and community representatives share in the decision-making process together with teachers and school administrators.[1] While the Carnegie School Program focused on public schools, its message of increased teacher influence is just as relevant for independent schools.

Sharing Decision Making With Students

A number of school systems throughout the United States are beginning to engage in the kind of school reform envisioned in the Carnegie School Programs, especially subscribing to a school-based management model in which there is a sharing of power together with increased accountability for the parties involved.[2] The thrust of much of this reform is for teachers to assume a more active and significant role in the decisions that are made in their schools and classrooms. I believe that teachers, working closely with administrators and parents, should have a large say in determining the curricula they teach, the books and materials they use for instruction, and the time allotted for different activities. However, as we consider who should participate in decision making in the schools, let us not neglect the other major group involved in the educational process—students. Obviously, the nature and extent of the decision-making powers delegated to students would have to be guided by students' developmental level, problem-solving capabilities, and interests.

I believe that the motivation and commitment of students will be heightened when they feel empowered, when they perceive that they are being heard and respected, and when they sense that they are having some influence in their schools. William Glasser, borrowing a concept from the field of business, has distinguished between educators who rely on two very different approaches with students, boss-management versus lead-management. Glasser characterizes *boss-management* as based on coercion, telling students what to do and how to do it. Glasser feels that the boss-management style contributes to an adversarial relationship among administrators, teachers, and students. In contrast, *lead-management* is predicated on shared problem solving and decision making. As Glasser notes:

> All students, both as individuals and as a group, could be asked to evaluate their classwork, homework, and tests and to put their evaluation of the quality of their work on everything they do. Just how they would do this would be discussed and agreed upon as part of the continual give-and-take in a lead-managed class. The constant aim would be to get the students involved in evaluating the quality of their own work. . . . A lead-manager emphasizes that problems are never solved by coercion; they are solved by having all parties to the problem figure out a better way that is acceptable to all. Because coercion is never an option, the lead-manager and the workers cannot become adversaries.[3]

To Support Autonomy

Having spoken with many educators, I have little doubt that learning and self-esteem will flourish in schools when a feeling of coercion is minimized, replaced by an atmosphere that supports autonomy and self-determination—a view shared by many others.[4] I believe that there are many ways in which teachers can encourage the active input of their students in solving problems and in contributing to decisions that impact on their education.

For instance, students can be engaged in developing and implementing class rules and regulations, in considering certain class projects such as deciding about a charity to support and how to raise money for a charity drive, or in reviewing books that might be purchased for the school library. As I will discuss in greater detail in the next chapter, the more we involve students in making decisions about school policy and procedures, the less likely they are to present disciplinary problems.

Many opportunities exist in schools for students to sharpen their problem-solving skills, to explore options, and to make decisions. For instance, in an elementary school a question was raised about whether students should be allowed to use their skateboards on school property. The administration referred the issue to the student council for consideration. The students discussed what information they needed in order to make a sound decision, which prompted conversations with lawyers, the police, and the chairperson of the town's Board of Selectmen to review the existing laws and the extent of the school's liability should an accident occur. Given what the students learned, they recommended that skateboards not be permitted on school grounds.

I am certain that in the process of confronting this issue about skateboards, the children's sense of competence was strengthened. In an interview in the *Boston Globe*, the principal of the school noted that "some people are afraid we're giving away our power to the kids. Others worry that, if given the chance to vote on school policy, students will abandon order and pass irresponsible rules. In fact, the opposite is true." The principal, who maintains veto power over the students' decisions, stated that he has not had to exercise this authority, observing that "so far the kids have been really great. I'm just an adviser willing to offer my wisdom whenever it's necessary."[5] Most students will act responsibly and maturely when treated with respect.

It is important to emphasize that when we involve students in problem-solving and decision-making tasks and when we provide input and assistance in a nonintrusive way, we reinforce skills that can be utilized in the acquisition of all kinds of knowledge, including different academic content. For example, as students discuss classroom rules—whether these rules pertain to homework being done on time or the scapegoating of other students—they are being engaged in a process that can enhance their ability to think in a reflective and flexible manner. As a consequence, the foundation is established for a more sophisticated way of thinking to emerge that can be applied to many different learning situations.

In addition, the reinforcement of problem-solving skills can be accomplished while teaching any school-related material, whether reading, math, social studies, science, music, or art. For instance, when children read a book, they can be asked to consider alternative ways that the main characters could have handled a certain situation. The same is true when discussing particular periods of history and the actions of different leaders. Problems in science and math lend themselves to defining hypotheses and thinking about strategies for testing these hypotheses in a clear and precise fashion. As teachers, you have the power to create the kind of school environment that has been recommended by Edward Deci, an expert in the field of motivation, an environment that takes as a top priority supporting the autonomy and competence of students. Deci and Cristine Chandler describe such an environment in the following way:

> Concretely, it means: using as little control as possible; encouraging children to think through their own problems rather than giving them solutions; permitting them to try out their own plans and ideas; and allowing them to work at their own speed. Pressuring them with rewards, tokens, deadlines, and prescriptions is counter to supporting autonomy.[6]

In support of this view, Deci and his colleagues found that the motivation, perceived competence, and self-esteem of fourth- through sixth-grade students increased when they were exposed to teachers who were rated high on the qualities of promoting autonomy rather than attempting to control what students did.[7]

As an educator and clinician, I continue to struggle with how best to motivate and teach, how best to provide feedback about performance, how best to have students learn strategies for approaching and solving problems. The style we use to instruct and to ask and answer questions is a significant variable in how effectively our students will learn problem-solving techniques. I remember a junior high school math teacher I had who skillfully responded to incorrect answers, not by immediately calling on another student or by coming across in a judgmental way, but rather by wondering how the problem might be solved. Not only did I learn about math from him, but as importantly, I learned about ways of solving problems and of being respectful.

As you think about your techniques for teaching and structuring a classroom, once more recall memories of your own teachers. Think about those teachers who turned the classroom into an environment that nurtured your abilities to confront and analyze issues and make sound judgments. What follows is a memory of such a teacher provided by an educator who completed my questionnaire:

> For two years, in the tenth and eleventh grades, I had an English teacher who truly challenged us to think and to form our own opinions about the books we were reading. He did this by never giving us his answers or opinions! This way we said what we believed, not what we thought he wanted us to believe. There were no "right" answers, only "valid" ones. You were allowed to voice any opinion—as long as you could support it from the book. We also sat in a circle, so the students were encouraged to discuss with each other, not look to him to direct. He also wrote lengthy comments on all our papers in addition to the grade. The comments were not only at the end but throughout the paper so you really knew he'd read it carefully! As for our grades, he always used to say, "Down you can't go. Sideways, maybe, but down you can't go." I have never forgotten this teacher . . . and to this day I consciously use his techniques when teaching my fourth graders.

This is truly a description of a self-esteem teacher, a teacher who has created a classroom in which students feel respected and empowered. We should attempt to emulate in our own unique manner what this teacher has accomplished, since in that way we will add to the dignity and self-worth of students.

Chapter Fifteen

TO ESTABLISH SELF-DISCIPLINE: THE BENEFITS OF CONSTRUCTIVE GUIDELINES AND CONSEQUENCES

"I remember when a teacher, after administering some tough discipline, took me aside and told me how much she cared for me."

"In the ninth grade, several of us decided to peroxide our hair and experiment with makeup in order to be like the girls at the high school. My English teacher took me aside one day and talked to me about what we now call 'peer pressure,' and the importance of building inner strengths as opposed to creating an 'image.' I had known him for several years, and seeing that he valued my academic strengths and personal qualities and cared enough to express concern was really important to me at the time."

I rarely give a presentation for teachers or parents that does not prompt questions about discipline. The questions are quite varied. "How do I stop my eight-year-old from hitting his four-year-old brother?" "How do I teach my child not to run into the street?" "How do I handle a temper tantrum?"

"What should I do if my child is not doing her homework?" "What should the punishment be if my daughter stays out beyond her curfew?" "Is there anything wrong with spanking my child once in a while?" "How do I get kids in the class not to tease each other?" "What's the best way to keep students from shouting out in class?" "How do I help students learn not to run in the classroom?" "How do I keep my students from swearing?" "What should I do when students don't do their assignments?"

The frequency and intensity with which these kinds of questions arise reflect how concerned we are about discipline, a concern that I believe is well deserved. In my experience, children with a positive self-image are typically children who possess a secure and comfortable sense of self-discipline. The emergence of self-discipline and self-esteem appear very interwoven.

What is inner discipline, or self-discipline? I view it as the ability to reason and make sound judgments, to reflect upon what we are doing, to think of the consequences of our behavior and the impact we have on others, to be respectful, and to assume responsibility and accountability for our actions. The words "secure and comfortable" were used in the previous paragraph to indicate that inner discipline is most effective when not burdened by feelings of guilt or by undue pressure.

The Emergence of Inner Discipline

Obviously, infants do not come into this world with a well-established sense of inner discipline. Self-discipline emerges slowly as a result of the dynamic, ongoing interaction between the developing cognitive and emotional skills of children and the thousands upon thousands of experiences that they encounter with parents, teachers, and other significant adults. Inner discipline is shaped in great part by the ways in which adults set limits, guidelines, and consequences for children.

We should never lose sight of the fact that when we discipline, we are involved in a process of education. Our goal is to assist students to become more thoughtful, responsible, and accountable and in the process to foster their self-esteem. Think about how you establish guidelines, expectations, limits, and consequences in your classroom. Do you always consider the developmental level of your students? Do you include them in the process of determining these rules and consequences? How would they respond if asked if the existing rules were fair? If your students were asked to describe your style of discipline, what words would they use? Would their words reflect feelings of respect, or resentment?

Walking a Tightrope

In establishing discipline in our classrooms, we are often required to walk on a tightrope, maintaining our balance between being too rigid and too permissive. As we engage in this balancing act, we should be guided by the belief that schools that mix warmth, nurturance, and acceptance with realistic expectations, clear-cut rules, and logical consequences are schools that are more likely to create a secure environment in which personal accountability, responsibility, learning, and respect can thrive. If we lean too much in one direction—holding expectations that are unrealistic, resorting to guidelines and rules that are rigid, and imposing consequences that are severe and demeaning— students will probably feel they are in a straitjacket with little room to grow. What does grow is their resentment and anger.

However, if we lean too much in the other direction, if we do not help provide reasonable expectations and guidelines, if consequences for one's actions are almost nonexistent, students will typically feel uncared for and confused. They will have difficulty learning responsibility, and feel frightened because of their lack of inner control, although this fright may be hidden behind such coping behaviors as angry outbursts or withdrawal. Given an absence of guidelines and consequences, our classrooms will be characterized by disorganization and uncertainty that will impact adversely on the learning that can take place.

I want to emphasize that caring and concern are communicated when rules and limits are established and discipline applied in a fair manner. For example, I recall a fourteen-year-old girl who entered therapy after having had an abortion. She told me that her parents had never set a curfew for her and that she could stay out as late as she wanted. As she came to trust me, she said that if her parents had set a curfew she would have fought them on it, but then she added with honesty and sadness, "But at least I would have known that they cared about me." This patient reminded me that caring is truly conveyed in many ways, including by establishing reasonable guidelines and consequences.

Discipline: A Story of Intervention and Prevention

As we struggle to walk on our tightrope and as we attempt to find the optimal balance for teaching responsibility, we should remember that discipline does not merely imply imposing a consequence for when students have transgressed. Instead, I learned years ago as director of the Psychoeducation Unit that discipline in the classroom is most effective when it moves beyond punishment and embraces a philosophy that includes as a top priority the prevention of behavior problems—especially when this prevention is accomplished by designing learning environments that actively promote the self-esteem of students.

When I first became director of the Psychoeducation Unit, most of our staff discussions centered on the kinds of consequences we should impose when patients acted out. In essence, we were trapped in a rigid, narrow crisis-intervention mentality, debating the effectiveness of different forms of punishment as we scurried from one crisis to the next. While I would never minimize the importance of articulating clear-cut consequences for disciplinary problems, I would argue that if the focus remains almost exclusively on crisis intervention, there will be little time or energy available for a staff to consider alternative measures for preventing disruptive behaviors and promoting a classroom climate conducive to learning. Also, when a staff is rushing from crisis to crisis, frustrations are apt to build, resulting in forms of discipline that tend to be punitive and serve to heighten students' resentment and lack of cooperation.

As I mentioned in my earlier discussion about coping behaviors, when students feel that their needs for self-determination, respect, competence, and belonging are thwarted, they are more likely to engage in counterproductive and disruptive activities. In adopting and placing greater emphasis on a crisis-prevention, compared with a crisis-intervention, approach, the Psychoeducation staff began to address the question of how best to help students—even within a locked-door unit—feel more of a sense of belonging and more in control of what transpired in the school.

I have already provided several examples of interventions that occurred when I was director of the Psychoeducation Unit, interventions that were guided by a crisis-prevention model rooted in the reinforcement of self-esteem (such as patients being able to schedule "special time" appointments with me and patients serving on the Space Committee to ensure that the environment was safe). These interventions helped produce a more secure, calm, constructive setting for learning. If you are able to implement at least several of the self-esteem strategies described in this book, you will be following a crisis-prevention approach. Within this approach, students are more likely to develop a strong alliance with you and less likely to engage in disruptive activities, since they feel they are being respected and empowered.

Prevention of Problems: Student Involvement in Decisions About Class Rules

In the previous two chapters, I emphasized the importance of students, with your guidance, having the power to make certain choices and decisions about their education. This decision making should extend as much as possible to the expectations, rules, and consequences that exist in the classroom. The process of discipline is most effective when students perceive consequences as logical and reasonable rather than as demeaning or belittling. I believe that involving students in the formation of rules and consequences that they experience as fair will facilitate the development of self-control and self-esteem.

How might students be involved in this process of determining rules and consequences? Imagine for a moment what might occur if at the beginning of the school year you engaged your students in a discussion about discipline by stressing that they had a significant responsibility for what transpired in the classroom and that it might be helpful to look at what rules were necessary for the classroom to function smoothly. During the discussion, you might ask if students thought rules were needed and what would happen if rules or guidelines did not exist. This kind of discussion can prompt students to discover the importance of having rules both inside and outside of school (for instance, at home or in Little League). The developmental level of your students will dictate the extent and nature of your input. My experience is that even kindergarten children can participate in a discussion about rules, and this involvement should be encouraged.

As you assist students to define class rules, the question of consequences can be addressed. You might say, "At times, any of us might forget the rules we have set and do something that is against a rule. How should we handle that when it occurs? What can we do if we keep forgetting a rule? If someone in the class forgets a rule, how will that make other students feel? What can we do to help all of us remember the rule in the future?" As the classroom teacher, you are in a position to guide without unduly directing or influencing the discussion as students consider different kinds of consequences. You can ask students to reflect on appropriate consequences based on the rule that is broken and on whether it is a particular student's first transgression.

You can also ask students to consider whether a rule should be changed.

The goal of having students deliberate about these questions is for them to gain an increasing sense of ownership for the rules and discipline that exist in the classroom. Obviously, you cannot anticipate all of the disciplinary issues that will arise in the course of a year, but if during the first few weeks of school you help create an environment in which the theme of discipline is an accepted topic for ongoing discussion, then any problem related to this theme can quickly be addressed.

Genevieve Painter and Raymond Corsini, in their thoughtful book about the use of discipline at home and in school, discuss the possible concern of finding time to engage students in a dialogue about classroom rules and consequences. They note:

> Many teachers feel that they cannot afford to take time away from academics for discussions. However, the time spent on guidance is generally a good investment. The class atmosphere improves and eventually more time becomes available for academics as behavior problems lessen. Some schools report fewer incidents of vandalism and that even students with delinquent behavior become cooperative when they are integrated into the group through regular classroom discussions.[1]

Once classroom rules and consequences have been established with the active participation of students, disciplinary problems should lessen. In addition, when such problems requiring disciplinary action appear, students can be referred to the procedures they have helped develop to determine what course of action to take. In this situation, well-defined, reasonable guidelines for student behavior will dominate the classroom scene, a classroom in which students understand and respect rules, in which they are less likely to perceive rules and subsequent disciplinary action as imposed upon them arbitrarily by adults, and in which they will assume increased responsibility, self-control, and accountability for their behavior.

Discipline and Our Teaching Styles

If you can stimulate this kind of classroom atmosphere, then, if misbehavior persists, you have a natural format for discussing the problem with students. The reoccurrence of misbehavior ought also prompt you to ask yourself if any of your classroom practices might be contributing to, or at least not helping to prevent, disciplinary problems. As I noted earlier in this book, we may have to change our own scripts, or standard ways of operating, to lessen the misbehavior and lack of motivation of our students. I have worked with teachers who have recognized that at times their expectations were too demanding and that they were disciplining students for small things. It is crucial for us to remember that we want students to see us as strong and caring, not as nagging or constantly watching for trouble.

I remember one fourth-grade boy who told me, "My teacher is always on my back. I can't do anything right." In fact, there may have been some truth to this perception, for the teacher shared with me how frustrated she was with this boy. Her frustration was evident in her reprimanding him in a seemingly harsh manner in front of the other children. (This reminded me of many similar negative memories offered by teachers on the anonymous questionnaire I distribute.) I knew that this boy could be quite provocative, especially when he was unable to do his schoolwork successfully and his self-esteem felt threatened. We used several self-esteem strategies to lessen his acting out, including having him tutor a younger child and, given his art talent, enlisting him in the design and creation of a large "Welcome Visitors" sign that was displayed at the entrance of the school. These strategies were aided by his teacher's recognition that in fact she was disciplining him in an angry fashion; subsequently, she made strides to be less angry and to select her areas of concern carefully.

An example of discipline being part of the educational process was in evidence in a middle school I visited, in which the assistant principal had students use detention time in a novel way. Rather than having students just sit and brood, he provided them with a list of approximately fifty topics related to the school or themselves and invited them to write a brief essay about one of these topics so that he could learn more about their experiences. I had the opportunity to read several essays and was very impressed with how constructively the students reflected upon their school and their lives. They truly learned from this form of discipline.

The self-esteem teacher is aware that discipline in the classroom is not synonymous with punishment and should not be permeated with remarks and actions that are demeaning and vindictive. Rather, if used effectively, discipline involves a process in which children carefully examine problems, make choices and decisions, work with other students and their teacher to develop classroom rules and consequences, and assume responsibility for what transpires in school. As these features of inner discipline are reinforced, so too is self-esteem. Motivation, accountability, and learning will flourish in such a classroom environment.

Chapter Sixteen

CONCLUDING REMARKS

"Mrs. K. made American history come alive to her eighth-grade students. She challenged us to really think about issues and rewarded us with little notes on top of our projects. More than any one encounter, she consistently showed us we were important and intelligent by her encouragement and enthusiasm."

"My sixth-grade teacher was my all-time favorite teacher! She was fun, and her class was fun to be in. She encouraged creativity, individuality, and above all, learning. We had made a full-scale papier-mâché model of John Glenn's space capsule, and had our parents and 'press' in for a panel discussion. She chose me to be Walter Cronkite, and when our question/ answer period was over, she told the audience that I was going to be the first woman astronaut. I wasn't, of course, but she made me feel like I could be. . . . I really loved her, and I think she's the one who made me decide to become a teacher."

Now that you have almost finished reading this book, I hope that you share my conviction of the significant role that you play in each student's life. You can be a self-esteem teacher, a charismatic adult who truly influences the paths that students follow. In your class today, you are creating the indelible memories that your students will hold for a lifetime, memories that are intimately tied to their self-esteem and their sense of well-being.

I hope that I have been able to capture how being a self-esteem teacher does not imply that you place the teaching of academic and other skills in the background or that you must add more work to your already busy schedule. The self-esteem strategies described in this book should go hand in glove with the material you are teaching. The use of these strategies should result in a more exciting classroom environment in which the motivation and satisfaction of your students are enhanced.

I want to emphasize again that the self-esteem strategies found in this book are but a few examples to illustrate the *Seeds of Self-Esteem* approach. While much of what has been said may seem obvious and simple, it can also be very subtle. Self-esteem teachers recognize that the impact they have on students may not always be apparent at first but can last a lifetime. That is why the *Seeds of Self-Esteem* approach aims to help you integrate what you teach with the way you teach. Such skill enables us to be more aware of not only shaping students' minds but of touching their spirits—the way they see and feel about themselves for the rest of their lives. Such influence is truly a rare privilege.

Footnotes

Chapter 1

1. Bednar, R., Wells, M., & Peterson, S. (1989).
*Self-Esteem: Paradoxes and Innovations in Clinical Theory
and Practice*. Washington, DC: American Psychological
Association; Frey, D., & Carlock, C. (1989). *Enhancing
Self-Esteem*. Muncie, IN: Accelerated Development.

2. California State Department of Education. (1990).
*Toward a State of Esteem: The Final Report of the Task Force
to Promote Self-Esteem and Personal and Social
Responsibility*. Sacramento, CA.

3. Borba, M., & Borba, C. (1978). *Self-Esteem: A
Classroom Affair*. Minneapolis: Winston Press; Canfield, J.
(1986). *Self-Esteem in the Classroom: A Curriculum Guide*.
Pacific Palisades, CA: Self-Esteem Seminars; Coopersmith, S.
(Ed.). (1975). *Developing Motivation in Young Children*. San
Francisco: Albion; California State Department of Education.
(1990). *Toward a State of Esteem: The Final Report of the
Task Force to Promote Self-Esteem and Personal and Social
Responsibility*. Sacramento, CA.; Reasoner, R. (1986).
Building Self-Esteem. Palo Alto, CA: Consulting
Psychologists Press.

4. DeFelice, L. (1989). The bibbidibobbidiboo factor in
teaching. *Phi Delta Kappan, 70*, 639-641.

Chapter 2

1. Segal, J. (1988). Teachers have enormous power in
affecting a child's self-esteem. *The Brown University Child
Behavior and Development Newsletter, 4*, 1-3.

2. *Ibid.*

3. Werner, E. (1990). *Against the Odds*. Ithaca, NY:
Cornell University Press.

4. Massachusetts Department of Education, Office of Student Services. (1988). *Systemic School Change: A Comprehensive Approach to Dropout Prevention*. Boston.

5. Kidder, T. (1989). *Among Schoolchildren*. Boston: Houghton Mifflin.

Chapter 3

1. Brooks, R. (1983). Projective techniques in personality assessment. In M. Levine, W. Carey, A. Crocker, & R. Gross (Eds.), *Developmental-Behavioral Pediatrics* (pp. 974-989). Philadelphia: Saunders.

2. Brooks, R. (1981). Creative Characters: A technique in child therapy. *Psychotherapy: Theory, Research and Practice, 18*, 131-139; Brooks, R. (1985). The beginning sessions of child therapy: Of messages and metaphors. *Psychotherapy, 22*, 761-769; Brooks, R. (1987). Storytelling and the therapeutic process for children with learning disabilities. *Journal of Learning Disabilities, 20*, 546-550.

3. White, R. (1959). Motivation reconsidered: The concept of competence. *Psychological Review, 66*, 297-333.

4. Bednar, R., Wells, M., & Peterson, S. (1989). *Self-Esteem: Paradoxes and Innovations in Clinical Theory and Practice*. Washington, DC: American Psychological Association; Gibbs, J. (1987). *Tribes: A Process for Social Development and Cooperative Learning*. Santa Rosa, CA: Center Source Publications; California State Department of Education (1990). *Toward a State of Esteem: The Final Report of the Task Force to Promote Self-Esteem and Personal and Social Responsibility*. Sacramento, CA.

5. Wechsler, D. (1974). *Wechsler Intelligence Scale for Children—Revised*. New York: The Psychological Corporation.

6. Brooks, R. (1981). Creative Characters: A technique in child therapy. *Psychotherapy: Theory, Research and Practice, 18*, 131-139.

Chapter 4

1. Weiner, B. (1974). *Achievement Motivation and Attribution Theory*. Morristown, NJ: General Learning Press; Brooks, R. (1990). Fostering self-esteem in the learning disabled child and adolescent: The search for islands of competence. *The Learning Consultant Journal, 11*, 28-33; Canino, F. (1981). Learned-helplessness theory: Implications for research in learning disabilities. *Journal of Special Education, 15*, 471-484; Dweck, C. (1986). Motivational processes affecting learning. *American Psychologist, 41*, 1040-1048; Schunk, D. (1982). Effects of effort attributional feedback on children's perceived self-efficacy and achievement. *Journal of Educational Psychology, 74*, 548-556.

Chapter 5

1. Brooks, R. (1984). Success and failure in middle childhood: An interactionist perspective. In M. Levine & P. Satz (Eds.), *Middle Childhood: Development and Dysfunction* (pp. 87-128). Baltimore: University Park Press.

2. Chess, S., & Thomas, A. (1987). *Know Your Child*. New York: Basic Books.

3. Coopersmith, S. (Ed.). (1975). *Developing Motivation in Young Children*. San Francisco: Albion.

4. Rosenthal, R. (1974). *On the Social Psychology of the Self-Fulfilling Prophecy: Further Evidence for Pygmalion Effects and Their Mediating Mechanisms*. New York: MSS Modular Publications.

Chapter 6

1. Chapman, W. (1991). The Illinois experience: State grants to improve schools through parent involvement. *Phi Delta Kappan, 72*, 355-358; Chrispeels, J. (1991). District leadership in parent involvement: Policies and actions in San Diego. *Phi Delta Kappan, 72*, 367-371; Davies, D. (1991).

Schools reaching out: Family, school, and community partnerships for student success. *Phi Delta Kappan, 72,* 376-382; Epstein, J. (1987). Parent involvement: State education agencies should lead the way. *Community Education Journal, 14,* 4-9; Epstein, J. (1991). Paths to partnership: What we can learn from federal, state, district, and school initiatives. *Phi Delta Kappan, 72,* 344-349; Solomon, Z. (1991). California's policy on parent involvement: State leadership for local initiatives. *Phi Delta Kappan, 72,* 359-362; Warner, I.(1991). Parents in touch: District leadership for parent involvement. *Phi Delta Kappan, 72,* 372-375.

2. Massachusetts Department of Education, Bureau of Student Development and Health. (1989). *Educating the Whole Student: The School's Role in the Physical, Intellectual, Social, and Emotional Development of Children.* Boston.

3. Solomon, Z. (1991). California's policy on parent involvement: State leadership for local initiatives. *Phi Delta Kappan, 72,* 359-362.

4. Epstein, J. (1987). What principals should know about parent involvement. *Principal, 66,* 6-9.

Chapter 7

1. Canfield, J. (1986). *Self-Esteem in the Classroom: A Curriculum Guide.* Pacific Palisades, CA: Self-Esteem Seminars; Reasoner, R. (1986). *Building Self-Esteem.* Palo Alto, CA: Consulting Psychologists Press.

2. Gaudino, A., & Tamaren, M. (1975). Learning through giving. *Instructor, 85,* 122-123.

3. Johnson, D., Johnson, R., & Holubec, E. (1988). *Cooperation in the Classroom.* Edina, MN: Interaction Book Company; Slavin, R. (1988). Cooperative learning and student achievement. *Educational Leadership, 45,* 31-33.

4. Gibbs, J. (1987). *Tribes: A Process for Social Development and Cooperative Learning*. Santa Rosa, CA: Center Source Publications.

Chapter 8

1. Adelman, H., & Taylor, L. (1990). Intrinsic motivation and school misbehavior: Some intervention implications. *Journal of Learning Disabilities, 23*, 541-550; Deci, E., & Chandler, C. (1986). The importance of motivation for the future of the LD field. *Journal of Learning Disabilities, 19*, 587-594.

Chapter 9

1. Rutter, M. (1980). School influences on children's behavior and development. *Pediatrics, 65*, 208-220.

Chapter 10

1. Greenspan, S. (1980). *A common framework for parent education: Bridging the gap between humanism and behaviorism*. Unpublished manuscript.

2. Rutter, M. (1980). School influences on children's behavior and development. *Pediatrics, 65*, 208-220.

Chapter 11

1. Brooks, R. (1988). Fostering self-esteem and caring: The taming of anger. In P. Vesin (Ed.), *Proceedings of the International Conference on Children and the Media: Channeling Children's Anger* (pp. 127-136). Paris: International Children's Center; Brooks, R. (1990). Indelible memories of school: Of contributions and self-esteem. *The School Field, 1*, 121-129.

2. Bronfenbrenner, U. (1979). *The Ecology of Human Development*. Cambridge, MA: Harvard University Press.

3. Rutter, M. (1980). School influences on children's behavior and development. *Pediatrics, 65*, 208-220.

4. Gaudino, A., & Tamaren, M. (1975). Learning through giving. *Instructor, 85*, 122-123.

5. Sarver, M. (1985). Agritherapy: Plants as learning partners. *Academic Therapy, 20*, 389-396.

6. Price, K., & Dequine, M. (1982). Peer tutoring: It builds skills and self-concept. *Academic Therapy, 17*, 365-371; Schrader, B., & Valus, A. (1990). Disabled learners as able teachers: A cross-age tutoring project. *Academic Therapy, 25*, 589-597.

7. Carnegie Council on Adolescent Development. (1989). *Turning Points: Preparing American Youth for the 21st Century*. New York.

8. *Ibid.*

9. Johnson, D., Johnson, R., & Holubec, E. (1988). *Cooperation in the Classroom*. Edina, MN: Interaction Book Company; Slavin, R. (1988). Cooperative learning and student achievement. *Educational Leadership, 45*, 31-33; it is well beyond the scope of this book to review the many different programs that fall under the umbrella of cooperative learning, but the reader is referred to the December 1989/January 1990 issue of *Educational Leadership* for a number of articles about this form of classroom learning. I am mentioning cooperative learning in this chapter since it requires students to work together in small groups and help each other achieve academic or social goals, or both.

10. Massachusetts Department of Education, The Division of School Programs and the Bureau of Student Development and Health. (1990). *Structuring Schools for Student Success: A Focus on Ability Grouping*. Boston.

11. *Ibid.*

12. Carnegie Council on Adolescent Development (1989). *Turning Points: Preparing American Youth for the 21st Century*. New York.

13. Slavin, R. (1989/1990). Research on cooperative learning: Consensus and controversy. *Educational Leadership, 47,* 52-54.

Chapter 12

1. Stargell, W. (1983, April 3). Yes, I am ready. *Parade Magazine,* pp. 10-12.

2. California State Department of Education. (1990). *Toward a State of Esteem: The Final Report of the Task Force to Promote Self-Esteem and Personal and Social Responsibility.* Sacramento, CA.

3. Meyer, A. (1983). Origins and prevention of emotional disturbances among learning disabled children. *Topics in Learning & Learning Disabilities, 3,* 59-70.

Chapter 13

1. Cohen, M. (1986). Intrinsic motivation in the special education classroom. *Journal of Learning Disabilities, 19,* 258-261.

Chapter 14

1. Massachusetts Department of Education. (1988). *Chapter 727, Carnegie Schools: Questions and Answers.* Boston.

2. Lieberman, A., & Miller, L. (1990). Restructuring schools: What matters and what works. *Phi Delta Kappan, 71,* 759-764; Watts, G., & McClure, R. (1990). Expanding the contract to revolutionize school renewal. *Phi Delta Kappan, 71,* 765-774.

3. Glasser, W. (1990). The quality school. *Phi Delta Kappan, 71,* 425-435.

4. Adelman, H., & Taylor, L. (1990). Intrinsic motivation and school misbehavior: Some intervention implications. *Journal of Learning Disabilities, 23,* 541-550; Deci, E., &

Chandler, C. (1986). The importance of motivation for the future of the LD field. *Journal of Learning Disabilities, 19,* 587-594; Dignan, P., & Schelkun, R. (1988, April). *Quality Circles go to school: Improving school climate through pupil, staff, and community involvement.* Paper presented at the annual meeting of the National Association of Elementary and Middle School Principals, San Francisco; Gibbs, J. (1987). *Tribes: A Process for Social Development and Cooperative Learning.* Santa Rosa, CA: Center Source Publications; Purkey, S., & Smith, M. (1983). Effective schools: A review. *Elementary School Journal, 83,* 427-452.

    5. Franklin, M. (1989, May 21). All kids in favor . . . *Boston Globe*, pp. 44-45.

    6. Deci, E., & Chandler, C. (1986). The importance of motivation for the future of the LD field. *Journal of Learning Disabilities, 19,* 587-594.

    7. Deci, E., Schwartz, A., Sheinman, L., & Ryan, R. (1981). An instrument to assess adults' orientations toward control versus autonomy with children: Reflections on intrinsic motivation and perceived competence. *Journal of Educational Psychology, 73,* 642-650.

Chapter 15

    1. Painter, G., & Corsini, R. (1990). *Effective Discipline in the Home and School.* Muncie, IN: Accelerated Development.

Bibliography

Adelman, H., & Taylor, L. (1983). Enhancing motivation for overcoming learning and behavior problems. *Journal of Learning Disabilities, 16*, 384-392.

Adelman, H., & Taylor, L. (1990). Intrinsic motivation and school misbehavior: Some intervention implications. *Journal of Learning Disabilities, 23*, 541-550.

Albert, L. (1989). *A Teacher's Guide to Cooperative Discipline: How to Manage Your Classroom and Promote* Self-Esteem. Circle Pines, MN: American Guidance Service.

Albert, L. (1990). *Cooperative Discipline: Classroom Management that Promotes Self-Esteem*. Circle Pines, MN: American Guidance Service.

Barth, R. (1990). *Improving Schools from Within*. San Francisco: Jossey-Bass.

Battle, J. (1981). Enhancing self-esteem: A new challenge to teachers. *Academic Therapy, 16*, 541-550.

Battle, J. (1982). *Enhancing Self-Esteem and Achievement*. Seattle: Special Child Publications.

Beane, J., & Lipka, R. (1986). *Self-Concept, Self-Esteem, and the Curriculum*. New York: Teachers College Press.

Bednar, R., Wells, M., & Peterson, S. (1989). *Self-Esteem: Paradoxes and Innovations in Clinical Theory and Practice*. Washington, DC: American Psychological Association.

Bloom, B. (1977). Affective outcomes of school learning. *Phi Delta Kappan, 59*, 193-198.

Borba, M., & Borba, C. (1978). *Self-Esteem: A Classroom Affair*. Minneapolis: Winston Press.

Briggs, D. C. (1970). *Your Child's Self-Esteem*. Garden City, NY: Doubleday.

Bronfenbrenner, U. (1979). *The Ecology of Human Development*. Cambridge, MA: Harvard University Press.

Bronfenbrenner, U. (1986). Alienation and the four worlds of childhood. *Phi Delta Kappan, 67*, 431-436.

Brookover, W., Beady, C., Flood, P., & Wisenbaker, J. (1979). *School Social Systems and Student Achievement. Schools Can Make a Difference*. New York: Praeger.

Brooks, R. (1979). Psychoeducational assessment: A broader perspective. *Professional Psychology, 10*, 708-722.

Brooks, R. (1984). Success and failure in middle childhood: An interactionist perspective. In M. Levine & P. Satz (Eds.), *Middle Childhood: Development and Dysfunction* (pp. 87-128). Baltimore: University Park Press.

Brooks, R. (1985). The beginning sessions of child therapy: Of messages and metaphors. *Psychotherapy, 22*, 761-769.

Brooks, R. (1987). Storytelling and the therapeutic process for children with learning disabilities. *Journal of Learning Disabilities, 20*, 546-550.

Brooks, R. (1988a). Adolescents and their families: Modifying anger and the "family script." In P. Vesin (Ed.), *Proceedings of the International Conference on Children and the Media: Channeling Children's Anger* (pp. 63-72). Paris: International Children's Center.

Brooks, R. (1988b). Fostering self-esteem and caring: The taming of anger. In P. Vesin (Ed.), *Proceedings of the International Conference on Children and the Media: Channeling Children's Anger* (pp. 127-136). Paris: International Children's Center.

Brooks, R. (1990a). Fostering self-esteem in the learning disabled child and adolescent: The search for islands of competence. *The Learning Consultant Journal, 11*, 28-33.

Brooks, R. (1990b). Indelible memories of school: Of contributions and self-esteem. *The School Field, 1*, 121-129.

Brooks, R. (1991). The learning disabled adolescent: A portrait. *Their World*, published by the National Center for Learning Disabilities, 27-31.

Brooks, R. (in press). Humor in psychotherapy: An invaluable technique with adolescents. In E. Buckman (Ed.), *The Handbook of Humor for Therapy*. Melbourne, FL: Krieger.

Brophy, J. (1986). Teacher influences on student achievement. *American Psychologist, 41,* 1069-1077.

California State Department of Education. (1990). *Toward a State of Esteem: The Final Report of the Task Force to Promote Self-Esteem and Personal and Social Responsibility.* Sacramento, CA.

Canfield, J. (1986). *Self-Esteem in the Classroom: A Curriculum Guide.* Pacific Palisades, CA: Self-Esteem Seminars.

Canino, F.J. (1981). Learned helplessness theory: Implications for research in learning disabilities. *Journal of Special Education, 15,* 471-484.

Carnegie Council on Adolescent Development. (1989). *Turning Points: Preparing American Youth for the 21st Century.* New York.

Carnegie Forum on Education and the Economy. (1986). *A Nation Prepared: Teachers for the 21st Century.* New York.

Chess, S., & Thomas, A. (1987). *Know Your Child.* New York: Basic Books.

Cohen, M. (1986). Intrinsic motivation in the special education classroom. *Journal of Learning Disabilities, 19,* 258-261.

Coopersmith, S. (1967). *The Antecedents of Self-Esteem.* San Francisco: Freeman.

Coopersmith, S. (Ed.). (1975). *Developing Motivation in Young Children.* San Francisco: Albion.

Davies, D. (1991). Schools reaching out: Family, school, and community partnerships for student success. *Phi Delta Kappan, 72,* 376-382.

Deci, E., & Chandler, C. (1986). The importance of motivation for the future of the LD field. *Journal of Learning Disabilities, 19,* 587-594.

Deci, E., Schwartz, A., Sheinman, L., & Ryan, R. (1981). An instrument to assess adults' orientations toward control versus autonomy with children: Reflections on intrinsic motivation and perceived competence. *Journal of Educational Psychology, 73,* 642-650.

DeFelice, L. (1989). The bibbidibobbidiboo factor in teaching. *Phi Delta Kappan, 70,* 639-641.

Dreikurs, R. (1964). *Children: The Challenge.* New York: Dutton.

Dweck, C. (1986). Motivational processes affecting learning. *American Psychologist, 41*, 1040-1048.

Epstein, J. (1987). Parent involvement: State education agencies should lead the way. *Community Education Journal, 14*, 4-9.

Feshbach, N. (1983). Learning to care: A positive approach to child training and discipline. *Journal of Clinical Child Psychology, 12*, 266-271.

Frey, D., & Carlock, C. (1989). *Enhancing Self-Esteem*. Muncie, IN: Accelerated Development.

Fulk, B., & Mastropieri, M. (1990). Training positive attitudes: "I tried hard and did well!" *Intervention in School and Clinic, 26*, 79-83.

Garmezy, N., & Rutter, M. (Eds.). (1983). *Stress, Coping, & Development in Children*. New York: McGraw-Hill.

Gaudino, A., & Tamaren, M. (1975). Learning through giving. *Instructor, 85*, 122-123.

Gibbs, J. (1987). *Tribes: A Process for Social Development and Cooperative Learning*. Santa Rosa, CA: Center Source Publications.

Glasser, W. (1986). *Control Theory in the Classroom*. New York: Harper & Row.

Glasser, W. (1990). The quality school. *Phi Delta Kappan, 71*, 425-435.

Glenn, S., & Nelsen, J. (1987). *Raising Children for Success*. Fair Oaks, CA: Sunrise Press.

Good, T., & Weinstein, R. (1986). Schools make a difference: Evidence, criticisms, and new directions. *American Psychologist, 41*, 1090-1097.

Goodlad, J. (1984). *A Place Called School: Prospects for the Future*. New York: McGraw-Hill.

Heyman, W. (1990). The self-perception of a learning disability and its relationship to academic self-concept and self-esteem. *Journal of Learning Disabilities, 23*, 472-475.

Johnson, D., Johnson, R., & Holubec, E. (1988). *Cooperation in the Classroom*. Edina, MN: Interaction Book Company.

Kent, M., & Rolf, J. (Eds.). (1979). *Primary Prevention of Psychopathology. Vol. III: Social Competence in Children*. Hanover, NH: University Press of New England.

Kidder, T. (1989). *Among Schoolchildren*. Boston: Houghton Mifflin.

Levine, M. (1987). *Developmental Variation and Learning Disorders*. Cambridge, MA: Educators Publishing Service.

Levine, M. (1990). *Keeping A Head in School*. Cambridge, MA: Educators Publishing Service.

Lieberman, A., & Miller, L. (1990). Restructuring schools: What matters and what works. *Phi Delta Kappan, 71*, 759-764.

Mack, J., & Ablon, S. (Eds.). (1983). *The Development and Sustaining of Self-Esteem in Childhood*. New York: International Universities Press.

Massachusetts Department of Education, Office of Student Services. (1988). *Systemic School Change: A Comprehensive Approach to Dropout Prevention*. Boston.

Massachusetts Department of Education, Bureau of Student Development and Health. (1989). *Educating the Whole Student: The School's Role in the Physical, Intellectual, Social and Emotional Development of Children*. Boston.

Massachusetts Department of Education, The Division of School Programs and the Bureau of Student Development and Health. (1990). *Structuring Schools for Student Success: A Focus on Ability Grouping*. Boston.

Meyer, A. (1983). Origins and prevention of emotional disturbances among learning disabled children. *Topics in Learning & Learning Disabilities, 3*, 59-70.

Nelson, R. (1989). Of Robin's eggs, teachers, and education reform. *Phi Delta Kappan, 70*, 632-638.

Painter, G., & Corsini, R. (1990). *Effective Discipline in the Home and School*. Muncie, IN: Accelerated Development.

Price, K., & Dequine, M. (1982). Peer tutoring: It builds skills and self-concept. *Academic Therapy, 17*, 365-371.

Purkey, S., & Smith, M. (1983). Effective schools: A review. *Elementary School Journal, 83*, 427-452.

Reasoner, R. (1986). *Building Self-Esteem*. Palo Alto, CA: Consulting Psychologists Press.

Rimm, S. (1986). *Underachievement Syndrome: Causes and Cures*. Watertown, WI: Apple Publishing.

Rosenthal, R. (1974). *On the Social Psychology of the Self-Fulfilling Prophecy: Further Evidence for Pygmalion Effects and Their Mediating Mechanisms*. New York: MSS Modular Publications.

Rosenthal, R., & Jacobson, L. (1968). *Pygmalion in the Classroom*. New York: Holt, Rinehart & Winston.

Rutter, M. (1980). School influences on children's behavior and development. *Pediatrics, 65*, 208-220.

Rutter, M. (1983). School effects on pupil progress: Research findings and policy implications. *Child Development, 54*, 1-29.

Rutter, M. (1987). Psychosocial resilience and protective mechanisms. *American Journal of Orthopsychiatry, 57*, 316-331.

Rutter, M., Maughan, B., Mortimore, P., Ouston, J., & Smith, A. (1979). *Fifteen Thousand Hours: Secondary Schools and Their Effects on Children*. Cambridge, MA: Harvard University Press.

Sarason, S. (1990). *The Predictable Failure of Educational Reform*. San Francisco: Jossey-Bass.

Sarver, M. (1985). Agritherapy: Plants as learning partners. *Academic Therapy, 17*, 365-371.

Schilling, D. (1986). Self-esteem: Concerns, strategies, resources. *Academic Therapy, 21*, 301-307.

Schrader, B., & Valus, A. (1990). Disabled learners as able teachers: A cross-age tutoring project. *Academic Therapy, 25*, 589-597.

Schunk, D. (1982). Effects of effort attributional feedback on children's perceived self-efficacy and achievement. *Journal of Educational Psychology, 74*, 548-556.

Searcy, S. (1988). Developing self-esteem. *Academic Therapy, 23*, 453-460.

Segal, J. (1988). Teachers have enormous power in affecting a child's self-esteem. *The Brown University Child Behavior and Development Newsletter, 4*, 1-3.

Sizer, T. (1984). *Horace's Compromise: The Dilemma of the American High School*. Boston: Houghton Mifflin.

Slavin, R. (1988). Cooperative learning and student achievement. *Educational Leadership, 45*, 31-33.

Slavin, R. (1989/1990). Research on cooperative learning: Consensus and controversy. *Educational Leadership, 47*, 52-54.

Strahan, D. (1989). Disconnected and disruptive students. *Middle School Journal, 21*, 1-5.

Warner, I. (1991). Parents in touch: District leadership for parent involvement. *Phi Delta Kappan, 72*, 372-375.

Watts, G., & McClure, R. (1990). Expanding the contract to revolutionize school renewal. *Phi Delta Kappan, 71*, 765-774.

Weiner, B. (1974). *Achievement Motivation and Attribution Theory*. Morristown, NJ: General Learning Press.

Weinstein, R. (1985). Student mediation of classroom expectancy effects. In J. Dusek (Ed.), *Teacher Expectancies* (pp. 329-350). Hillsdale, NJ: Erlbaum.

Werner, E. (1990). *Against the Odds*. Ithaca, NY: Cornell University Press.

White, R. (1959). Motivation reconsidered: The concept of competence. *Psychological Review, 66*, 297-333.

Other Seeds of Self-Esteem materials you'll find valuable for personal and classroom use . . .

Seeds of Self-Esteem Videos

Two videos (approx. 30 min. each) that vividly demonstrate the great and lasting impact teachers have on students' self-esteem. Robert Brooks and a host of real students and teachers lead you on a journey to becoming a self-esteem teacher. Use the videos for school-wide inservice training, for small group study, or individually. For educators in kindergarten through grade nine. (Each video includes a video guide.)

Video 1

Self-Esteem Teacher Power: Topics include Teacher Impact, The Student's Point of View, and Attribution Theory.

Video 2

Self-Esteem Teacher Strategies

The Self-Esteem Teacher's Journal

Here are dozens of helpful activities for using self-esteem skills in your classroom. This 112 page journal is your personal map or plan that lets you adapt all of the ideas you've read about in the *Teacher's Handbook* to your own style. Includes a planning calendar, ideas from teachers on how to implement strategies, and take-home activities.

Posters

These colorful posters feature appealing graphics, photography, and illustrations that invite student participation in activities keyed to esteem building themes. They provide support, ideas, and guidance to fully implement the program in the classroom—or schoolwide. Three levels are available (primary, upper elementary, and middle school/junior high); each level includes nine full-color posters.

TO ORDER, WRITE:
AGS, 4201 Woodland Road, Circle Pines, MN 55014-1796
Or call toll-free 1-800-328-2560

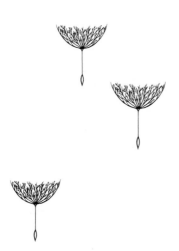